COMMAND CONTROL

for Toy Trains

— **Second Edition** —

Neil Besougloff
revised by Carl Swanson

KALMBACH BOOKS

Kalmbach Books
21027 Crossroads Circle
Waukesha, Wisconsin 53186
www.Kalmbach.com/Books

Published in 2009
13 12 11 10 09   1 2 3 4 5

Manufactured in United States of America

ISBN: 978-0-89024-752-5

Cover photos: front – Lionel model no. 28577 CP Rail GP30 diesel
locomotive; back – MTH model no. 20-3345-1 *Orient Express* 2-3-1
Pacific steam engine, courtesy of MTH

Publisher's Cataloging-In-Publication Data

Besougloff, Neil.
  Command control for toy trains / written by Neil Besougloff ; revised by
Carl Swanson. -- 2nd ed.

  p. : ill. ; cm.

  Includes index.
  ISBN: 978-0-89024-752-5

1. Railroads--Models--Electronic equipment. 2. Digital control systems.
I. Swanson, Carl A., 1960- II. Title.

TF197 .B48 2009
625.1/9/0284

Lionel®, LEGACY™, RailSounds®, TrainMaster®, and TMCC® are
trademarks of Lionel Trains L.L.C., Chesterfield, Michigan.

M.T.H.®, DCS™, Proto-Sound® 2.0, and RailKing® are trademarks of
M.T.H. Electric Trains, Columbia, Maryland.

This book is neither authorized nor approved by Lionel Trains L.L.C. or
M.T.H. Electric Trains.

Introduction

In a 2007 survey, readers of *Classic Toy Trains* magazine selected command control technology as the biggest trend of recent years in the toy train industry.

Command-control operation of locomotives and layouts is no longer the future of O gauge model railroading – it is the present.

The goal of this book is to help new and existing operators without technical backgrounds better understand command-control systems designed to operate O gauge trains.

To keep the information within the grasp of all O gauge operators, MTH's Digital Command System and Lionel's Legacy and TrainMaster Command Control components are explained in down-to-earth terms. My apologies to those looking for a technical analysis.

Both MTH and Lionel are continually improving their command-control products. When I wrote the first edition of this book in 2002, MTH's DCS had just debuted and TMCC's second-generation Legacy controller was only in the discussion stages at Lionel.

Today, Lionel's Legacy products are on store shelves and MTH has upgraded its DCS software numerous times. Both companies promise more to come as hobbyists continue to embrace the digital age of O gauge model railroading.

—*Neil Besougloff*

Command control history **1**

For more than 70 years, train control remained the same: operators controlled trains by varying the flow of electricity to the track with a transformer.

Operating toy trains is all about control, but for nearly a century, the flow of electricity to a piece of track, not the train itself, was all that could be controlled.

Raise the track voltage and the train went faster. Put an additional train on the track and it went faster as well. There was no way to individually control the speed of each train because both would blindly respond only to the amount of voltage sent to the track.

The dawn of cab control

As model railroading moved away from a living-room oval to a dedicated model railroad, the concept of cab control developed. Pioneering scale model railroaders divvied up layouts into separate electrical segments, or blocks. While the rails appeared to run seamlessly from one block to the next, each block was electrically insulated from the others. Each block had a toggle switch to select between one transformer, called a cab, or another. Through deft manipulation of toggle switches as trains moved from block to block, two operators could independently control the speed and direction of two different trains on the same layout. That is, as long as the two locomotives were not in the same block at the same time. If they were, both would speed up or slow down together. Cab control was still controlling the track and not the trains.

Control by magic

Just before World War II, Lionel tried a different, less sophisticated and, ultimately, less satisfying tactic. Called Magic

Electrol, it was a two-train set powered by alternating current. It did not allow independent control of locomotive speed, but it allowed each locomotive to move forward or backward independently of the other. While one locomotive followed standard toy train protocol (forward, neutral, reverse, neutral), the reverse unit of the second locomotive was controlled by direct current added to the AC track power.

With Magic Electrol, operators pressed a whistle button, but instead of triggering a whistle relay, the direct current triggered a relay connected to a special reverse unit. Lionel's catalogs proudly announced that independent control had arrived. Well, short-lived independent direction control anyway, since Magic Electrol did not return when Lionel renewed train production in 1946 after World War II.

Voice-activated control

Direction control was also the focus of Marx's Radio Tower. Shout "stop" into the tower as if it were a microphone, and a running train powered by an ordinary transformer would stop. Shout "reverse" and it would back up. Magic? No. The tower contained a diaphragm wired to the track power. Shouting into the tower moved the diaphragm, which interrupted the track power and cycled the locomotive's reverse unit.

The Electronic Set

Just after World War II, Lionel produced its Electronic Set, the grandfather of today's command control. While the Electronic Set did nothing to advance independent two-train control, it did, for the first time, offer cordless push-button activation of a number of O gauge train features – a whistle, coil couplers, a reverse unit, and even a dump car – independently of one another.

Each car in the Electronic Set had a radio receiver mounted to its frame. When a push-button control box transmitted the proper radio signal, the receiver was activated and triggered a relay. In concept, Lionel's Electronic Set shared much with today's TrainMaster Command Control. But in the years just after World War II, vacuum-tube technology was unreliable, and keeping radio signals in proper tune was a headache. Also, the Lionel set was especially expensive, and it disappeared after a few years.

Introduced by Lionel in 1995, this Denver & Rio Grande Western SD50 was an early TMCC-equipped locomotive (6-18221).

A big gap
While the Marx Radio Tower and similar diaphragm-operated devices would soldier on through the 1950s, and Digital Command Control of HO and other scale model railroads would be developed and popularized in the 1960s, '70s, and '80s, there were no new developments in independent control of AC-powered O gauge trains until 1994.

Enter rock star Neil Young. Millions know him for his music, and the O gauge community knows he was instrumental in the development of Lionel's TrainMaster Command Control. Announced in 1994, TrainMaster Command Control, TMCC for short, was everything the developers of Magic Electrol, the Electronic Set, and even Marx's Radio Tower dreamed of – and more.

Then, in 2002, a second command control system became available when MTH Electric Trains introduced its Digital Command System (DCS) And in 2008, Lionel brought out Legacy, its second-generation TMCC system.

2 Command control basics

A command-controlled locomotive responds to commands when addressed by the controller.

Conventional control is control of the power in your track. You can turn power on or off, raise or lower power, and interrupt power to cycle O gauge trains to neutral or reverse. In conventional mode, whether you have one locomotive or 10 on your track, they all respond in unison to the power changes you make to the track.

Command control is control of the locomotives on the track. In command-control mode, the voltage on the track has a constant setting, usually 18 volts. The voltage does not increase or decrease as you turn the command-control throttle up or down. Each command-controlled locomotive contains a receiver with a unique numerical code called an address. Only when a locomotive "hears" its address called by the command-control components will it respond. For example, if you have two locomotives on your track, numbers 16 and 67, locomotive number 16 will only respond to commands specified for locomotive 16, and locomotive 67 only to commands specified for locomotive 67. If you don't use the proper address, the locomotives will not move an inch.

TMCC and DCS
Lionel's TrainMaster Command Control (TMCC) and MTH's Digital Command System (DCS) are multiple-component command-control systems designed for AC-powered O gauge trains, although they work equally well in other scales and gauges utilizing AC power. Both feature wireless handheld

controllers that send signals to a base station. From the base station, the signals are sent to the track and, ultimately, to the locomotives. By assigning unique addresses to locomotives, both systems allow you to operate multiple trains independently on the same layout at the same time.

Both systems also have the ability to turn special effects on and off with the handheld controller. Special effects can include numerous train-related sounds, exterior and interior locomotive lighting, electrically controlled couplers, and joining locomotives in a lash-up with a single command. TMCC and DCS can also throw track switches and turn accessories on and off remotely.

The command control systems also allow you to switch between conventional-control mode and command-control mode, so locomotives without receivers can operate on the same layout by raising and lowering track voltage with a handheld controller.

The differences between DCS and TMCC

DCS and TMCC perform the same functions, but they use different paths to achieve those functions.

TMCC's handheld controller sends a radio signal to a base station. In command-control mode, the base station uses the outside rails of the track as a broadcast antenna to send a second radio signal to the locomotives. And an antenna inside each TMCC-equipped locomotive then picks up the signal. Lionel signals are broadcast at the same frequency as citizens band radio transmissions.

When operating in conventional-control mode, TMCC's handheld controller also sends a signal to a base station. That signal raises and lowers the track voltage according to input given to the handheld controller.

DCS's handheld controller also sends a signal to a base station, using the same frequency as a 900-megahertz cordless telephone. In command-control mode, the digital signal sent from the DCS handheld controller to the base station is mixed into the AC power going to the track. Locomotives with DCS receivers hear their signals as they pick up power directly from the center rail of the track. Unlike Lionel's system, the MTH signal is not independent of the track power.

When operating in conventional-control mode, DCS's handheld controller also sends a signal to the base station that raises and lowers track voltage accordingly.

The CAB-2 and the DCS controller have a similar design that includes buttons, soft keys, and a display screen.

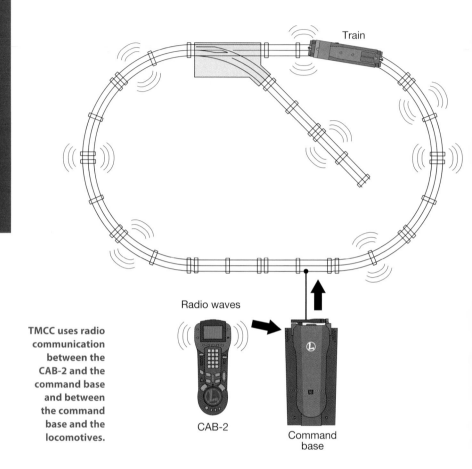

Train

Radio waves

CAB-2

Command
base

TMCC uses radio communication between the CAB-2 and the command base and between the command base and the locomotives.

ProtoSound 2.0 and RailSounds

TMCC and DCS integrate locomotive sound effects with command-control functions. Lionel's sound system is called RailSounds, and most, but not all, TMCC-equipped locomotives have RailSounds. MTH combines its command control and sound into one package called ProtoSound 2.0.

TMCC components

Lionel's TMCC family of components has grown regularly since 1994. Some components are new, such as Lionel's Legacy command base and CAB-2 handheld controller, which arrived in 2008. Others are upgrades of existing components. In 2001, Lionel bought IC Controls' line of TMCC products and integrated it into its own line, which created some overlap. To help TMCC customers select the proper

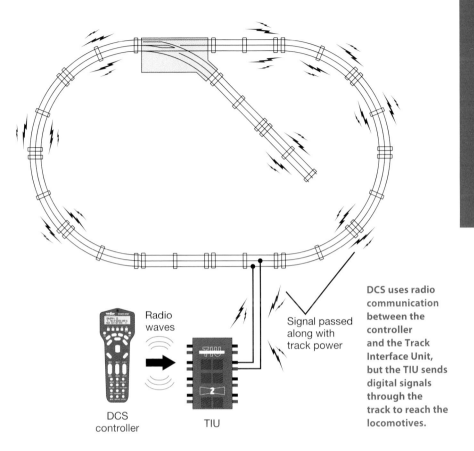

Radio waves

Signal passed along with track power

DCS controller

TIU

DCS uses radio communication between the controller and the Track Interface Unit, but the TIU sends digital signals through the track to reach the locomotives.

components, Lionel labeled the overlapping products with a description of good, better, or best.

To operate in command mode, TMCC requires a handheld controller, either the original CAB-1 or the Legacy system's CAB-2, and the corresponding command base. For basic command-mode operation, nothing more is needed.

To operate TMCC in conventional mode as well as command mode, a third component called a PowerMaster is needed. The PowerMaster raises and lowers track voltage by listening to the command base.

In addition to the PowerMaster (good), you can also use a TPC 300 (better) or TPC 400 (best). Both TPC models are more expensive than a PowerMaster but offer more features and can handle much larger-capacity transformers. (TPC stands for Track Power Controller.)

TMCC-controlled switches and accessories

A number of other Lionel TMCC components add enhancements beyond basic command and conventional control. Lionel makes the SC-2 track switch controller and the Accessory Switch Controller (ASC). Both can throw track switches and turn accessories on and off through commands from either a CAB-1 or Legacy CAB-2 handheld controller. The Accessory Motor Controller (AMC), operates motor-driven accessories, such as a gantry crane or log loader, and the Accessory Voltage Controller (AVC) is used to fine-tune the voltage given to accessories.

Other components include the Block Power Controller (BPC), Operating Track Controller (OTC), Action Recorder Controller (ARC), and the Big Red Control Button. The BPC acts as a traffic cop routing power to different electrical blocks on large layouts and lessens the need for extra Power-Masters or TPCs. The OTC operates remote control or uncoupler sections of track. The ARC can record handheld controller keystrokes and repeat them, in effect recording train movements for later identical playback. The Big Red Control Button dates from the beginning of TMCC. When pressed, it repeats the handheld controller's most recent input.

DCS components

While a sophisticated TMCC layout might use 10 or more TMCC components all with unique functions, DCS packages many of those functions into just two components, the Track Interface Unit (TIU) and the Accessory Interface Unit (AIU). Lionel's Legacy also combines some features as well.

To operate DCS in either command-control mode or conventional-control mode, you need the DCS handheld controller (it doesn't have a specific name) and the TIU. The AIU throws track switches and turns accessories on and off.

Power supply

Both the DCS and TMCC systems need an outside power supply. You can use a transformer of any vintage that will produce alternating current at a constant 18 volts. A transformer must also have enough wattage to power two or more locomotives simultaneously.

Lionel makes 135-watt and 180-watt PowerHouse transformers specifically for TMCC. Lionel's new ZW transformer, a modern interpretation of the postwar ZW transformer, uses the same PowerHouse transformers. The ZW is designed for command control as well as conventional control, and it contains some of the same circuitry as a PowerMaster component.

MTH does not make a specific transformer for DCS, but the company suggests using its 400-watt Z-4000 transformer.

If using an older transformer, such as a postwar Lionel or American Flyer transformer, you'll likely need additional circuit protection. Postwar transformer circuit breakers probably will not respond fast enough to protect the sensitive electronics inside the TMCC and DCS components.

Using an existing layout

TMCC is the less demanding of the two systems to install in an existing layout. The system broadcasts signals to locomotives by using the outside rails of the track as a radio antenna, so dirty track or electrical blocks of track (whether controlled by toggle switches or relays) rarely cause any signal reception problems.

DCS is slightly more demanding when installed in an existing layout. Since the DCS signal rides with the track power through the center rail to a locomotive's pickup rollers, dirty track, combinations of toggle- and relay-controlled blocks, and even common-ground wiring can weaken signal strength.

3 The right system for you

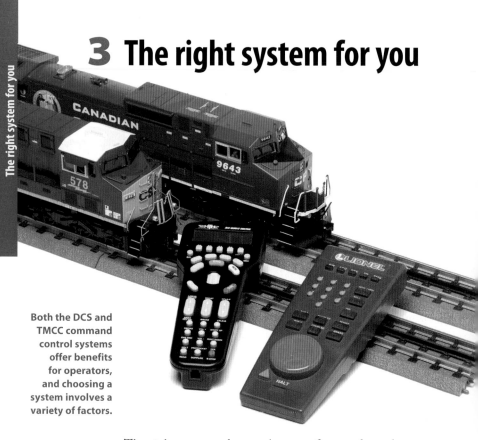

Both the DCS and TMCC command control systems offer benefits for operators, and choosing a system involves a variety of factors.

The right command control system for you depends on a variety of factors including your layout, your wallet, your preference in trains, your comfort level and degree of patience with electronics, and how you operate trains.

Creating a checklist

To help determine if you are better suited for TMCC or DCS, you can create a checklist using these five factors. Add up your check marks, think again about what you like and don't like, make your decision, and then take the plunge.

Adding command control to your layout

If you have an existing medium- or large-sized layout full of electrical blocks, relays, and toggle switches, TMCC can be added with less work. Adding DCS could involve rewiring sections of your layout using the star wiring method.

If you plan to build a new layout, DCS might be easier to install. Using star wiring is recommended by MTH and not difficult to master (see page 74). Also, DCS components are a snap to connect to each other and there are far fewer of them.

Command control system costs

Both Lionel and MTH offer their command systems in packages or as separate components.

You can purchase MTH's DCS handheld controller and Track Interface Unit together for about $300. Adding an Accessory Interface Unit would add about another $100. DCS software upgrades can be downloaded from MTH's Web site.

Lionel's Legacy set, with a CAB-2 remote controller and a command base, costs about $300. A PowerMaster (to enable conventional control) and other TMCC components would be extra.

A TrainMaster Command Control set, with a CAB-1 controller and a command base, runs about $150. Adding a PowerMaster or Track Power Controller would cost another $80 to $200. An Action Recorder Controller ($100) and other components add to that total. The costs can add up quickly.

When determining overall costs, don't forget to include any locomotives you wish to add.

MTH's broad line of RailKing locomotives, all of which are now equipped with ProtoSound 2.0, starts at $250 for a diesel engine. At the higher end, MTH's Premier line locomotives with ProtoSound 2.0 begin at around $400, and some steam engines will top $1,000.

Lionel locomotives that are TMCC-equipped can be purchased starting at about $370. Those that are Legacy-equipped range from $400 to more than $1,000 for a high-end locomotive.

Your preference in trains – and brands

If you are a loyal Lionel customer and only buy an occasional MTH locomotive that you don't mind operating only in conventional-control mode, then put a check mark in the TMCC column. If you're a dedicated MTH fan, the check mark goes in the DCS column.

Your comfort level with electronics

If you use your personal computer or PDA daily, surf the Internet with your cell phone, and enjoy listening to an MP3 player, DCS gets the check mark for its two-way communication and ability to operate TMCC-equipped locomotives in command mode.

If you use the word *newfangled* often and have never visited YouTube or Facebook, you might prefer operating the original Lionel CAB-1 system.

Like DCS, the Lionel CAB-2 Legacy system involves a bit of a learning curve to unlock all its capabilities.

You can operate both DCS and TMCC systems and locomotives on the same layout, as does the Central Operating Lines O gauge club of Long Island.

How you operate trains

How you operate trains may be the final deciding factor between DCS and TMCC. Does your layout have a freight yard? Do you do a lot of switching? Do you have enough track to create routes? Do you bounce back and forth between conventional- and command-control modes? Do you operate prewar and postwar trains? Do you just sit back and watch?

DCS, with its scale mph readouts and feature-laden menus, gives you a better taste of prototype railroading in command-control mode.

TMCC, however, has superior conventional-mode control, making it the more balanced of the two systems, and the Legacy system has its own neat Official Railroad Speeds feature.

A simple toggle switch can send power from a TIU to TMCC components.

The best of both worlds

If you can't decide on one system, you can have it both ways and use DCS and TMCC on the same layout.

You can blend DCS and TMCC on one layout. There's nothing to prevent you from building a DCS layout and then adding a command base and a CAB-1 or CAB-2. You can also use a Lionel PowerMaster or TPC on a DCS layout for finer conventional-control operation. You can use a high-amperage double-pole, double-throw switch to toggle transformer power from your TIU to your TMCC components.

Conversely, you can use the same thinking to add DCS to an existing TMCC layout.

System components 4

To operate a TMCC-equipped locomotive, you'll need a CAB-2 or CAB-1 and a command base.

To add Lionel TMCC to your layout, you'll need either a first-generation CAB-1 or a second-generation Legacy CAB-2 handheld controller, the appropriate command base for your handheld, and at least one locomotive equipped with TMCC.

The handheld controller

In addition to unlocking all the features of Legacy-equipped locomotives, the CAB-2 can control any TMCC-equipped locomotive, and it even uses the same numeric command sequence as those used in original CAB-1 operation. The Legacy CAB-2 differs from the original in that it has a multifunction LCD screen along with a number of advanced operating features, many of which only apply to Legacy-equipped locomotives.

The CAB-2 resembles an overgrown television remote control. The 3¾" x 9¼" device is powered by three recharge-able AA batteries that recharge when the CAB-2 is placed on the base station's cradle.

The CAB-2 has a multifunction LCD screen and offers more advanced operating features than does the CAB-1.

Located directly below the CAB-2's LCD screen are five rectangular soft keys. These keys correspond to the five selection boxes at the lower part of the display screen. Normally, they control the system's most-commonly used functions:

The most commonly used keys of the CAB-1 are also found on the CAB-2.

- SW to address track switches
- ACC to address accessories
- RTE to address prerecorded track switch routes
- TR to address tracks or a lash-up of locomotives
- ENG to address locomotives

For basic train operation, you will use the TR and ENG buttons most often.

The same five buttons are found on the original CAB-1, but the Legacy soft keys are also used to select options in the system's Info/Options menu. A touch-screen keypad is located below the row of soft keys. This screen changes to display either numerals or a series of icons, depending on which set of functions are selected.

The numerals are used to address prenumbered locomotives, accessories, track switches, track sections, and routes. The icons control a wide range of features, including sound, locomotive smoke, momentum, and a selection of preset speed ranges.

Left of the touch-screen pad is the CAB-2's train brake slider that is used to apply greater or lesser amounts of brake force. To the right of the pad is a similar sliding switch that controls the locomotive bell and the variable (on Legacy-equipped locomotives) train whistle or horn.

Other buttons on the CAB-2 include a combined speed boost, brake, and direction control; large square buttons for front and rear couplers; and a pair of buttons labeled Aux-1 and Aux-2 that control the direction in which track switches are set and the locomotive lighting and control panel views.

Next to the Aux-2 button is the red triangular Halt button. The Halt button overrides all commands to locomotives and accessories on the track and kills power to the track.

At the very bottom of the CAB-2 are four more buttons: Set, L, M, and H.

The round, red throttle dial

Last, but certainly not least, is the round, red throttle dial. Unlike traditional transformer handles, which have clearly defined Start and Stop positions, the handheld's dial spins in endless circles. There is no notch to indicate zero or maximum because TMCC operates the locomotives not the track. A single controller can operate many different locomotives at once, each at a different speed. If there were notches on the throttle dial, it would be impossible to shift on the fly between different locomotives operating at different speeds. An endlessly spinning dial is a necessity if you want to operate different locomotives moving at different speeds with a single controller.

The command base

The Legacy CAB-2 sends its radio signal to a command base. The 5½" x 10¾" command base has an antenna, a power jack, a computer interface port (reserved for future applications), an On/Off switch, a channel selection button, and a binding post for a wire between the command base and the outside rail of the track.

When the command base receives signals transmitted by the CAB-2, it broadcasts a second signal through the wire

The command base receives radio signals from the CAB-2.

connected to the outside rail of the track. That signal is sent throughout your layout using the outside rails of your track as a broadcasting antenna. Antennas within each TMCC-equipped locomotive receive those signals and respond just to the signals sent to the locomotive's numeric address. If signals are sent to locomotive number 16, only locomotive number 16 will respond.

In a way, operating TMCC in command-control mode is like operating two connected radio stations, each with a transmitter and a receiver.

Conventional control

To operate prewar, postwar, and any other non-TMCC-equipped locomotives on your layout using a CAB-1 or CAB-2 instead of a conventional transformer handle, you need another component. Lionel offers three choices: the PowerMaster, the Track Power Controller (TPC) 300, and the TPC 400.

Why use TMCC to operate trains in conventional mode? Although there are no command-control features, you do have a wireless walk-around throttle and much finer speed control of locomotives on the track. Most throttles work in a linear way – movement of the throttle in equal increments causes the track voltage to raise or lower in equal increments. Not so with TMCC. Its electronic throttle is weighted at the low-speed end of the scale. More increments at lower speeds means more control.

In addition, Lionel's TMCC uses a modified AC wave form. When viewed on an oscilloscope, the high and low

The TPC 400 is the best power distribution choice.

PowerHouse transformers plug into the back of a modern ZW transformer.

portions of the TMCC wave are flattened, or chopped. At low rpms, Lionel's open-frame Pullmor motors are more responsive to this chopped wave.

PowerHouse transformers

The final piece needed for basic TMCC operation is a transformer. Lionel makes two transformers specifically for TMCC – the 180-watt PowerHouse and an older 135-watt PowerHouse.

Nicknamed bricks, PowerHouses are different from other O gauge transformers. PowerHouses are either on, providing 18 volts AC, or they are off. There is no handle to vary their voltage output. This suits TMCC perfectly. In command mode, PowerHouses provide a constant 18 volts directly to the track. In conventional mode, a PowerHouse feeds into a PowerMaster or TPC, where track voltage is regulated by turning the handheld controller's red dial.

Other transformers

Any transformer that supplies AC power at 18 volts can be used, and transformers with modern circuit protection are recommended. Non-PowerHouse transformers require Lionel's power adaptor cable since the input side of the PowerMaster uses a uniquely shaped, three-prong plug. Regardless of the output wattage of your transformer, the PowerMaster will only supply 135 watts to the track. The TPC 300 and TPC 400 are capable of handling 300 and 400 watts, far more than a PowerMaster.

Lionel's ZW transformer

Lionel's modern ZW transformer has a control case that looks just like a postwar ZW. But power comes from one to four remote PowerHouse transformers plugged into the back of the case of the ZW. The ZW operates in conventional-control mode as a traditional transformer, and in command-control operation, it substitutes for both the power supply and the PowerMaster or TPC.

TMCC buyer's guide

Here is a list of Lionel's TMCC components and their part numbers:

- Legacy Command Set (6-14295):
  CAB-2 (991) and command base (992)

- Trainmaster Comand Set (6-12969):
  CAB-1 (6-12868) and command base (6-12911)

- PowerMaster (6-24130)

- Track Power Controller 300 (6-14189)

- Track Power Controller 400 (6-14179)

- 180-watt PowerHouse (6-22983)

- Accessory Switch Controller (6-14182)

- SC-2 Switch Controller (6-22980)

- Accessory Motor Controller (6-14183)

- Accessory Voltage Controller (6-14186)

- Action Recorder Controller (6-14181)

- Block Power Controller (6-14184)

- Operating Track Controller (6-14185)

TMCC-equipped locomotives 5

Legacy-equipped locomotives, such as this CP Rail GP30 (6-28577), will operate in both conventional- and command-control modes.

All TMCC and Legacy locomotives can be operated in either conventional-control or command-control modes. In conventional-control mode, the locomotives operate just like prewar and postwar locomotives: they respond to changes in track voltage and cycle between forward, neutral, and reverse. No special commands, programming, or equipment is necessary for conventional-control operation.

In command mode, locomotives must be assigned a number, or address. The Legacy system offers four ways to select a locomotive. You may address the engine by its identification number, road number, or name, or you can simply toggle through the available engines using the display screen.

Legacy-equipped locomotives are sold with a small memory module that transfers the locomotive's road number, railroad name, and list of available options for that Legacy engine when the chip is inserted into a CAB-2. The system reverts to CAB-1 mode (basic TMCC) unless you insert the memory module or manually enter options for that Legacy locomotive. The system should retain this

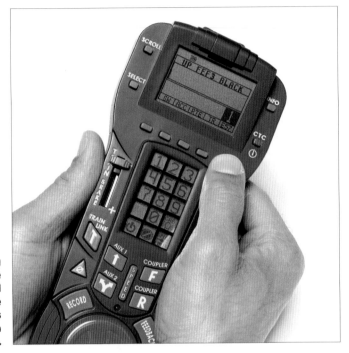

Addressing a locomotive through its road name is one of four ways to address a locomotive.

information but keep the modules in a safe place in case they are needed.

To load an engine memory module into the memory, address the Legacy-equipped engine by its identification number, press Info, select Load Module using the soft keys, insert the memory module into the slot on top of the CAB-2, and then follow the on-screen directions.

Once assigned an address, TMCC locomotives are ready for command-control operation.

How does a locomotive know?

How does a locomotive know if it should operate in conventional-control mode or command-control mode? On a conventional-control layout, there is no command base to send signals through the rails. Without a TMCC signal, the TMCC locomotive defaults into conventional-control mode operation and responds only to changes in track voltage.

If, however, the locomotive detects a TMCC signal from the command base, the locomotive starts up in command-control mode and will only respond when it is addressed, regardless of the voltage being sent to the track.

Memory modules fit into the slot at the top of the CAB-2.

Enhancements over the years

The first group of TMCC locomotives offered command control of locomotive direction, speed, and basic RailSounds features. While the horn, whistle, or bell of any RailSounds-equipped locomotive can be activated in conventional-control mode, command-control mode offers control of diesel locomotive rpm rates (revs for short) and startup and shutdown sounds. In later models, you can also control the voice of a dispatcher, coupler opening sound effects, and radio chatter.

Also in later models, Lionel began to add remote-activated couplers to its TMCC locomotives. The couplers themselves are very much like the coil couplers of the early postwar years. But instead of being dependent on track activators to open, TMCC coil couplers open with a command-control signal from the handheld controller.

The arrival of Legacy TMCC in 2008 added better speed control for all TMCC locomotives, a display screen, a wide range of command improvements, and new features. For example, the CAB-2 shakes gently to simulate the laboring of a locomotive.

Newer and modular circuit boards

Today's TMCC circuit boards are smaller in size, offer additional features, and are more modular in construction. They plug into sockets in locomotive frames and into RailSounds circuit boards. Modular construction reduces production costs and simplifies repair.

Lionel's use of modular circuit boards created a series of command-ready Lionel locomotives. Command-ready locomotives have sockets that accept TMCC and Rail-Sounds circuit boards, but they do not come with the actual boards. Out of the box, these locomotives can only be run in

TMCC circuit boards

Locomotives from Atlas O and other manufacturers contain factory-equipped circuit boards for TMCC operation.

conventional-control mode, but you can easily add a modular TMCC or RailSounds board and a TMCC antenna to these locomotives to give them full command capabilities.

Non-Lionel TMCC-equipped locomotives

Atlas O, Weaver, and other manufacturers regularly offer locomotives factory-equipped with Lionel's TMCC and Rail-Sounds circuitry. Their components are as reliable as those in Lionel locomotives.

All non-Lionel TMCC-equipped locomotives operate in either conventional-control mode or command-control mode, just as Lionel's own TMCC locomotives do. But not all offer the full line of TMCC features such as coil couplers, infrared tethers between steam locomotives and tenders, and remote smoke control. Also, a locomotive may or may not use a Rail-Sounds system that perfectly matches the prototype. Before you buy one, check its features by examining the locomotive and reading the instructions.

At time of publication, Lionel has not made its new-generation Legacy locomotive boards available to other manufacturers; however, the Legacy CAB-2 controller can operate any TMCC-equipped engine from any manufac-turer, although, obviously, no Legacy-specific features can be activated.

Adding TMCC to your layout 6

Even on small layouts, TMCC offers excellent train-control features.

TMCC can be put on any new or existing toy train layout, from a 4 x 8-foot oval to the most sophisticated museum-sized layout.

Small layouts

On smaller layouts, such as an oval with sidings on a sheet of plywood, two or more TMCC-equipped trains operating independently at the same time may simply not fit. It's no fun operating nose-to-tail with collisions all but inevitable.

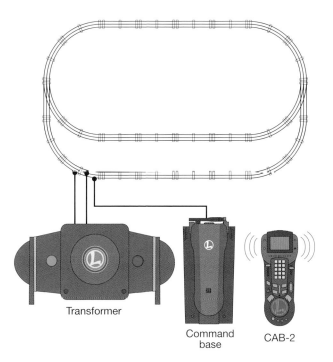

Transformer

Command base

CAB-2

Wiring a TMCC system on a small layout is simple.

But TMCC still gives operators of small layouts walk-around control over locomotives, accessories, sound, and other effects that would otherwise be impossible. It also allows you to park locomotives on sidings without turning off power to the sidings or physically lifting a locomotive off the layout. It gives you more speed increments when operating in conventional mode. And on a small layout, there is no need to divide the track into electrical blocks – one power source is enough.

Medium layouts

TMCC excels on medium-sized layouts, those 8 x 12-foot or larger. There is room enough to run two or three trains at once without bumping into one another, yet the power needs of such a layout can be met by a single, although large, transformer that can power a single electrical block with multiple track power

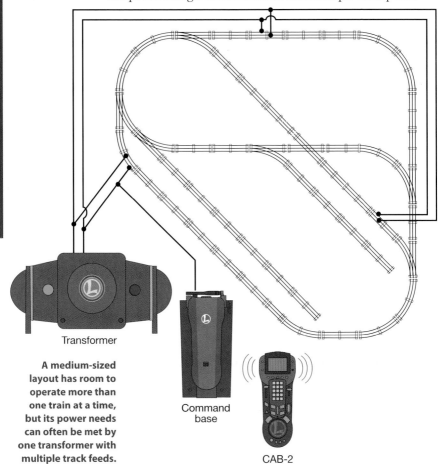

Transformer

A medium-sized layout has room to operate more than one train at a time, but its power needs can often be met by one transformer with multiple track feeds.

Command base

CAB-2

feed wires. If you operate power-hungry locomotives like those with old-style Lionel Pullmor motors, a second or third power block can be added with minimal additional wiring.

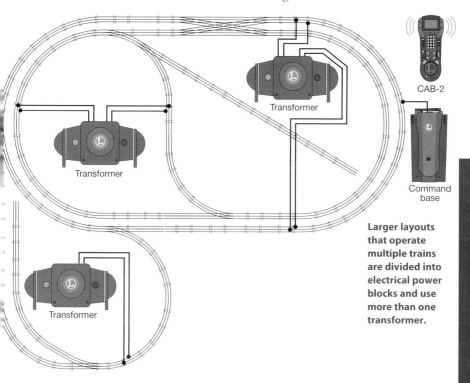

CAB-2

Transformer

Command base

Transformer

Transformer

Larger layouts that operate multiple trains are divided into electrical power blocks and use more than one transformer.

Large layouts

Expansive layouts, such as those that fill an entire basement or a dedicated train room, are proportionately more sophisticated. But TMCC can control the entire layout from a single handheld controller and eliminate a panel filled with rows of transformers, toggle switches, and accessory controllers.

Large TMCC layouts must be divided into electrical blocks to keep five, six, seven, or a dozen or more locomotives supplied with enough power. The power needs are no different from those of a similar-sized layout without TMCC.

Large layouts require multiple PowerMaster or TPC components in relation to the number of electrical blocks and multiple track switch and accessory control units. But even the largest layouts follow the very same setup and operation principles as a 4 x 8-foot TMCC layout.

Electrical blocks

Medium- and large-sized layouts, those designed to run more than four trains at once, need independent electrical blocks. One 135-watt or 180-watt Lionel PowerHouse transformer can power two or three trains at once, but usually no more. Larger transformers can put out more power, but they also have a finite limit when powering an entire layout.

The concept of electrical blocks – dividing a layout into sections, each with its own power supply – has been in use since the early days of electric trains. A block has a plastic pin or other insulating material at each end of the center rail, electrically separating the power (hot) rail of the block from the rest of the layout. The two outside rails, supplying the return (ground) voltage, are not insulated. Doing so would keep the TMCC signal from being broadcast the entire length of your layout.

All the transformers powering the electrical blocks must be in phase, meaning that their power and ground wiring is all aligned. In-phase transformers share the same common wire, yet by insulating the center rail of each transformer's block, the power and its voltage sent to that block won't dissipate across the entire layout.

Breaking up a medium- or large-sized TMCC layout into electrical blocks allows all of the trains to receive full power when required since it is highly unlikely that all of the trains will be bunched onto the same electrical block of the layout at the same time. Ideally, your layout would have about the same number of blocks as the usual number of trains running.

More powerful than a single locomotive

The maximum output of one PowerMaster is 135 watts, even if you use a larger transformer like a 180-watt PowerHouse or a 275-watt postwar ZW. While 135 watts to a single electrical block is sufficient to operate two modern, can-motored trains at once, it is barely enough to keep two Pullmor-motored locomotives and their trains, especially passenger cars full of lights, going at the same time.

The TPC 300 can output 300 watts of power to the rails in a single block, and the TPC 400 can output 400 watts. Either is plenty for a single electrical block, and using the full 400-watt capacity of the TPC 400 in a single block should be left to those with expertise in electricity. You can use a transformer with less than 300 or 400 watts and still benefit from a TPC.

How many watts?

If you really want to know how large a transformer you need, take the time to calculate how much power your layout requires. This list, drawn from postwar Lionel instruction books and reviews of locomotives in *Classic Toy Trains* magazine, will help.

The wattage amounts listed for Lionel Pullmor-motored locomotives include the power drawn by their lights. Modern can-motored locomotives draw roughly half the power, but fan-driven smoke units and sound systems often make up the difference. For ampere draw, divide these numbers by 15.

Locomotive with single motor 60

Locomotive with single motor, whistle, and smoke 90

Locomotive with dual motors 105

Motor-powered accessories 20-25

Vibrotor-powered accessories 10-20

12-volt light bulb (each) 3

18-volt light bulb (each) 5

Light bulbs and accessories

Traditionally, toy trains operate between zero and 18 volts, although some prewar and postwar transformers actually top out closer to 24 volts. Lionel chose 18 volts as the optimum voltage level for TMCC layouts and designed its TMCC circuits to work best at 18 volts.

While ideal for motor power, 18 volts is hard on lighted passenger cars and other rolling stock and accessories that are powered by track voltage. Most toy train bulbs are designed to operate between 12 and 18 volts. If possible, replace all of your bulbs with 22-volt or 24-volt ones.

Your layout's wiring

An adequately wired layout can handle 18 volts continuously and upwards of 4 amps per train without generating excessive heat. Wire gauge numbers work backwards, so the smaller the numerical gauge, the larger the wire's diameter. Small TMCC layouts should use 20 or 18 (preferred) gauge wire, medium-sized layouts should use 18 or 16 gauge wire, and larger layouts should use 16, 14, or even 12 gauge wire. The gauge you choose also should be determined by the length, or run, of the wires. Longer runs mean greater electrical resistance. To overcome increased resistance on a run of 12 feet or more, use the next larger sized wire.

Connect wires between components and the track through a terminal block for easy wiring.

Installing TMCC train-control components

TMCC wiring for command operation requires a handheld controller, a command base, one wire, and an electrical outlet. An additional connection is needed to operate your layout in conventional-control mode using the original CAB-1 or the Legacy CAB-2 handheld controller.

To set up a CAB-2, insert the three rechargeable AA batteries supplied with the Legacy system, set it on the command base, and allow it to charge for at least 30 minutes.

The command base has two connections, which are the only connections needed for basic command-control mode operation if you have an existing transformer that can be set to a constant 18 volts.

For its power, the command base connects to a wall transformer, similar to one used for a telephone answering machine. It also connects to the outside track rail with a wire from the thumbscrew terminal binding post on the end of the command base. The command base receives radio signals from the handheld controller and sends a second radio signal to the track through the U terminal wire.

Three rechargeable AA batteries power the CAB-2.

Included with the Legacy system are three memory modules that plug into the top of the CAB-2 to load basic system information. Individual Legacy locomotives also have memory modules that include information specific to the features found on that particular locomotive.

Connecting a PowerMaster or TPC

To operate trains in conventional mode using the CAB-1 or CAB-2, you'll need to connect a Lionel PowerMaster or a

Track Power Controller (TPC) to your layout. The Power-Master or TPC raises and lowers track voltage in response to the movements of the handheld controller's dial.

The PowerMaster is placed electrically between the transformer and the track. You connect it with three wires: one paired wire from the transformer to the PowerMaster and two separate wires, one hot and one ground, from the PowerMaster to the track.

The TPC uses one more connection than a PowerMaster, and this connection allows the TPC to talk to the command base. The additional connection is made with a computer serial-style cable. One end of the cable has a DB9 connector that fits into the socket marked Computer on the command base. Red and green wires on the other end connect to the Dat (data) and Com (common) signal terminals on the TPC.

Dat and Com signal terminals each connect with a single wire.

Using a ZW transformer

Lionel's ZW transformer, a modern version of its iconic postwar transformer, can also be used on a TMCC layout in both command-control and conventional-control modes using either the ZW throttle arms or the CAB-1 or CAB-2 dial to control trains.

On the outside, the modern ZW looks like its postwar counterpart, but inside it has components that take the place of a PowerMaster. Power for the ZW actually comes from an external source, one to four PowerHouse transformers identical to those designed for TMCC.

Because the ZW can utilize up to four PowerHouse transformers, each assigned to its own block, it makes a good all-in-one alternative for a medium-sized TMCC layout using up to four electrical blocks. Be aware, though, that the new ZW's ability to control trains through each of its four throttles, or through the CAB-1 or CAB-2 red dial, can cause confusion for novice operators.

A ZW transformer can control up to four blocks.

7 Operating TMCC locomotives

A locomotive will start up in command-control mode if it hears a TMCC signal.

Once a command base is plugged in and its U terminal is attached to an outside rail of your track, you're ready to operate in command-control mode.

First, make sure your TMCC locomotive is in Run mode. On most locomotives, the Run/Program slide switch is on the underside of the frame. On diesel locomotives, the switch is usually on the outer edge of the frame near the front truck. It's a black switch on a black frame, so look closely. Some locomotives also have similar-looking smoke On/Off switches

The Run/Program switch is often found on the frame of a diesel locomotive.

on their undersides. On steam locomotives, the Run/Program switch is usually on the tender frame, but it may be partially hidden by one of the trucks.

The Program position is used to change the two-digit address of the locomotive. Brand-new TMCC locomotives leave the factory with number 1 as their address (also known as an ID number).

Place your locomotive on the track and make sure the command base is plugged in before you raise the track power to 18 volts. The locomotive will start up in command-control mode if it hears the TMCC signal. If you turn up the track power before turning on the command base, the locomotive will start up in conventional-control mode.

Adding a PowerMaster

A PowerMaster or Track Power Controller (TPC) on your layout allows you the flexibility to operate, in conventional-control mode, postwar or other non-TMCC locomotives using the wireless handheld controller instead of the handles of a transformer.

Using a PowerMaster or TPC adds another step to command-control operation. Since the PowerMaster or TPC controls track voltage, you must send a command to either of those components to turn on the track voltage. If you are using a PowerMaster, move the slide switch to Cmd. This sets the PowerMaster to an all-or-nothing mode – all is 18 volts and nothing is zero volts. Press TR on the handheld controller, press the PowerMaster ID number, usually number 1, and then press Boost. Now you have 18 volts on the rails and can proceed to address your locomotive.

Adding a TPC

The TPC 300 and TPC 400 are addressed differently from the PowerMaster. Instead of a moving a slide switch between command and conventional control, you use the buttons on the bottom of the handheld controller. The buttons are Set, L, M, and H. When addressing a TPC, L indicates command mode, M indicates conventional, and H is not used.

To command the TPC to put 18 volts into the track, press TR, press the address or ID of the TPC, press L, and then press Set.

The buttons at the bottom of a CAB-2 are used to address a TPC.

The buttons on a CAB-1 are found under a small access panel.

Addressing the locomotive

You should now have the command base on, the track power at 18 volts, and a locomotive at rest on your layout awaiting a command. To address a locomotive with a CAB-1, press ENG, enter the locomotive's ID number, and press Boost.

For a Legacy CAB-2 controller, tap the ENG or TR buttons to access the addressing touch-screen display, enter the engine ID, and press Start Up. (This button is at lower left on the touch pad and has the international symbol for a power switch, a circle with a bar at the top.) Remember, your locomotive was given the address of 1, not 01, at the factory. You'll hear a growl from the diesel locomotive RailSounds speaker or a whoosh from a steam locomotive speaker. Turn the red dial clockwise, and congratulate yourself – you're operating in command-control mode.

Changing the locomotive's address

Changing addresses is easy if you have Legacy-equipped locomotives. Once you have entered the locomotive's name and options, either manually or using the engine's memory module, the identification information is already in the CAB-2.

If you are running a basic TMCC locomotive and add another one to your layout, you'll need to change the address of at least one of the locomotives; otherwise, you cannot operate each locomotive independently because they'll both have factory address 1.

To change the address of a TMCC locomotive, you must remove all locomotives from the track except the one needing

---

Remembering addresses

The new Legacy system makes it easy to remember locomotive addresses. Once you've loaded that information, either manually or using the memory module supplied with a Legacy locomotive, the information is stored and can be readily accessed using the display panel.

Things are a little trickier with the original TMCC CAB-1 system. As you build your engine roster, the chance of forgetting numbers grows.

One way to remember addresses is to write them down on a checklist stored near your CAB-1. Another, easier way, is to use the first two numbers on the locomotive's cab as its address. For example, a no. 5433 Hudson steamer is assigned address 54, and a no. 1999 diesel has address 19. You may also opt to assign a memorable number like 99 as a particular locomotive's address.

a new address. Move the Run/Program slide switch on the underside of the locomotive or tender to Program. Put the locomotive on the track and turn on the track power. Press ENG, enter the new address or ID number, and then press the Set button. Your locomotive now has a new address and will confirm the address change by a blow of the whistle or horn. Turn off the track power, slide the switch back to Run, and you're ready to go.

That big, red throttle dial

The red throttle dial, without any fixed starting or stopping points, is probably unlike any you have used before. The throttle is designed this way, so you can jump from one command-control locomotive to another without the second locomotive jumping immediately to the speed of the first.

The red throttle dial has no start or stop marks.

Also, the increments of acceleration and deceleration (Lionel calls these speed steps) are not evenly spaced. The nonlinear design of the increments, weighted toward low-end speeds, gives you greater throttle control at slower speeds.

Turning the red throttle dial clockwise increases speed until your locomotive is at its top speed, which is equivalent to your locomotive operating at 18 volts in conventional mode. The display screen provides speed information, including a momentum bar that shows your progress as the train works its way up to the speed you've selected.

In addition to the red dial, the CAB-2 also has preset railroad speeds corresponding to 5, 20, 35, 50, and 70 miles per hour. Activate them by pressing Speed and the desired speed on the touch screen. There is also a button that takes you straight to maximum speed.

Turn the red dial counterclockwise to slow and stop your locomotive. (You can also use the CAB-2's sliding train brake lever.) If you turn the red dial clockwise after a stop, your locomotive will move out in the same direction.

Changing direction

Press the direction (DIR) button once, and your locomotive is poised to reverse direction, but it won't begin to move in the opposite direction until you turn up the throttle dial.

There is no neutral in command mode. When your locomotive slows to a stop, the TMCC circuitry reaches a point where it turns off the locomotive's electric motor or motors, but the circuitry itself remains powered to operate the sound system, smoke unit, and other features.

Pressing the DIR button at speed won't slam the locomotive into wheel-screeching reverse. The locomotive will slow down to a stop, waiting for a turn of the red dial before moving out in the opposite direction.

The CAB-1 Boost button controls a variety of functions.

The CAB-2 slider operates bells, horns, and whistles.

Brake and boost controls

The brake lever gradually slows the speed of your train, with the emphasis on gradual. It's most useful in mimicking prototype operations, such as arriving at a passenger station. As you brake to a stop, you must hold the brake slider. Taking your finger off the slider causes the locomotive to accelerate at a moderate rate to its previous speed.

The original-style CAB-1 controller includes a Boost button. When pressed, it increases acceleration until the button is released, at which time the train resumes normal speed. On TMCC steam locomotives with RailSounds, pressing Boost also produces a labored chuffing sound.

The CAB-1 Boost button has a secondary TMCC function. It acts as a Start or Enter key when starting up your locomotives. Press ENG, the locomotive's ID number, and then Boost to wake up your TMCC locomotive.

Toot-toot, honk-honk, and ding-ding

The CAB-2 slider controls one of the neatest features of Lionel's new-generation Legacy system. The locomotive's horn or whistle is blown when the slider is moved downward. You can ring the locomotive's bell once by pushing the slider upward and quickly releasing it; push it up and hold it slightly longer before releasing it, and the bell will sound continuously. To cancel the bell, push the slider upward and release.

Other RailSounds effects

RailSounds uses standardized keystrokes to activate or modify sounds. Not all locomotives have the same features, so not all keys respond the same with every RailSounds locomotive.

The volume can be changed by pressing ENG, entering the ID number, and pressing the up or down keys on the touch pad. You can also engage dispatcher and crew talk effects or shut down RailSounds entirely.

For Legacy-equipped locomotives, the touch screen displays icons for controlling the engine RPM sounds, setting the smoke unit on or off, and even (for Legacy steam engines) controlling water injector and steam blow-down sounds.

Non-Legacy TMCC locomotives offer some of these same options, which are controlled by a numerical key pad. For example, you can operate the smoke unit in steam locomotives and in diesel locomotives equipped with smoke units. Set the CAB-2 to CAB-1 (original TMCC) mode, press ENG, enter the ID number, and press number 8 and then number 9 on the touch pad.

Coil couplers

Lionel knuckle couplers with a built-in electrical coil were first manufactured more than 55 years ago. The knuckles on those couplers opened when electricity from a special track section energized the coil.

The coil couplers available on newer TMCC-equipped locomotives use the same design principle, but they are energized through the TMCC circuitry, not a special section of track. The coil couplers can be opened anywhere on a layout at any time. There are two buttons on the handheld controller marked Coupler. The F button opens the front coupler, and the R button opens the rear. Pressing the Coupler button not only opens the coupler, it produces a satisfyingly loud whoosh followed by a mechanical snap sound.

Jumping between locomotives

You can operate as many TMCC-equipped locomotives at once as you can handle, switching back and forth between them at will. Pressing ENG and the ID number moves you between different locomotives on the fly. An easy way to know which locomotive you are controlling is to tap the Whistle/Horn button, and the locomotive under control will blow or honk at you.

Turning off your locomotive

There are two ways to turn off TMCC locomotives and the 18 volts of power to your layout. You can use a controlled stop or a panic stop.

Controlled stops. Under normal circumstances, shutting down your layout is a two-step process – shutting down loco- motives and then shutting down the track. To shut down your locomotives, stop their movement using either the throttle dial or the DIR button. Then, for locomotives with RailSounds, press the stop-sign-shaped icon on the CAB-2 touch screen (or the Aux-1 key at the bottom of the CAB-1 and then the number 5 key). This initiates the RailSounds shut-down sequence, which is the equivalent of shutting off your car in the driveway. Besides the audio gratification, it shuts down the RailSounds circuitry in its designed sequence.

Turn off the track power after all of the active locomotives have been turned off. If your layout uses only a command base and traditional transformer, simply turn off the track voltage and unplug the transformer.

If your layout uses a PowerMaster or TPC, you need to press TR, the track ID number, AUX-1, and then the 0 key. The PowerMaster or TPC then turns off the 18 volts of power on the rails, but you still must turn off or unplug your layout's transformer.

Panic stops. When collisions or derailments are inevitable, pressing the triangular, red Halt button stops everything. The Halt button kills all commands, and locomotives will stop as if someone pulled the transformer plug out of the wall. On the CAB-1, it is located at the bottom of the controller, and on the CAB-2, it is above the Record button. On layouts equipped with a PowerMaster or TPC, pressing the Halt button also kills track voltage, which is a big advantage of running your 18 volts of track power through a PowerMaster or TPC.

Pressing the Halt button on the CAB-1 brings everything to a stop.

TMCC reprogramming codes

At times, TMCC-equipped locomotives may need to be reset if they run erratically or don't run. Follow these seven steps to reprogram a locomotive:

1. Move the Run/Program switch to Program.

2. Turn on the command base.

3. Place the locomotive on the track and turn up the power.

4. Press ENG, the locomotive's address number, and then Set.

5. Turn off the power and wait 10 seconds.

6. Pick up the locomotive and move the Program/Run switch back to Run.

7. Place the locomotive back on the track, turn up the power, and address the locomotive.

Use this list of reprogramming codes for some older TMCC-equipped Lionel locomotives.

Code	Locomotive
0	Steam with Signal Sounds
1	Diesel with Signal Sounds
2	Diesel with cab light and Signal Sounds
4	Steam with smoke
5	Diesel with strobe light (GP7, GP9, GP20)
6	Diesel with cab light (PB-1, FT, F3)
8	Diesel with smoke
34	6-2800 series Hudson, Pacific, K-4, and West Side Shay steam
36	Alco PA (1997), WP, NYC, and Texas Special F3
74	All locomotives with wireless tether (except J1E and SF Warhorse)
75	Soo Line SD-60
740	J1E Hudson and SF Warhorse
750	Conrail Dash-8, 1999 Centennial SD-40
760	BNSF Dash-9 (6-18235)

8 Conventional control

TMCC provides precision control of postwar steam locomotives.

Although command-control operation is most popular, operating conventional-mode trains using a TMCC handheld controller and TMCC components offers advantages as well. TMCC is backward-compatible with almost any AC-powered O gauge locomotive made by Lionel or other manufacturers. Older MTH locomotives equipped with that company's original ProtoSound control and sound system may need help, however (more about that later).

Also, TMCC provides finer control of conventional locomotives, especially postwar and prewar locomotives with Lionel Pullmor and similar open-frame motors, because of its modified electrical wave pattern and large number of conventional-control speed increments. Even Marx, prewar American Flyer, and Ives O gauge motors run more smoothly.

Control your entire layout

You can control track switches, accessories, and track blocks using a Legacy CAB-2 or an original CAB-1 handheld controller, regardless of whether you operate locomotives in command-control or conventional-control mode. On a TMCC layout operated in conventional-control mode, components such as the SC-2 track switch and accessory controller, the Accessory Switch Controller (ASC), and the Accessory Motor Controller (AMC) remain just as useful.

TMCC components including the ASC, SC-2, Block Power Controller (BPC), and Operating Track Controller (OTC), alone or by triggering separate relays, can take the place of toggle or rotary switches that turn on and off electrical blocks and sidings. They can also take the place of push buttons used to activate uncoupler track sections and animated rolling stock such as a milk car or a log dump car.

TMCC and original ProtoSound

In the mid-1990s, operators discovered that some, but not all, MTH locomotives equipped with the original Proto-Sound system (not the newer ProtoSound 2.0 system) did not operate properly in conventional-control mode on TMCC-equipped layouts using a Lionel PowerMaster. Early production ProtoSound locomotives would turn on their sound systems but otherwise wouldn't budge. Later ProtoSound locomotives would respond to forward, neutral, reverse, and throttle-speed commands, but their sound systems would be mute. While other ProtoSound locomotives would exhibit only a few of these traits, some of the last original ProtoSound production locomotives from 1998 and 1999 ran just fine.

In conventional-control mode, original ProtoSound circuitry at its start-up, when sensing TMCC's modified electrical wave, promptly shut down the locomotive completely, partially, or not much at all on TMCC-equipped layouts. In time, MTH modified its electronics to make their products run smoothly on TMCC layouts under conventional control. Other solutions were also developed.

QS Industries, which designed the original ProtoSound system with MTH, offered a conversion circuit board that removed incompatibility issues on early ProtoSound locomotives. The QS-3000 circuit board even unlocked some nifty MTH sound effects normally reserved for users of MTH's Digital Command System. But using the QS-3000 necessitated modification to each and every original ProtoSound locomotive, an expensive proposition.

When using a Track Power Controller, the TPC filters the TMCC electrical wave to make it acceptable to ProtoSound-equipped locomotives. With a TPC, originally developed by Lou Kovach of IC Controls, incompatibility is all but eliminated. However, you may encounter a stubborn early ProtoSound-equipped locomotive that simply doesn't get along with TMCC.

TPC and ProtoSound programming

Both the TPC 300 and TPC 400 offer benefits beyond basic compatibility to operators of MTH ProtoSound locomotives. You may use a CAB-1 or CAB-2 numeric keypad with a TPC to start a ProtoSound-equipped locomotive and properly bring it out of its initial rest mode. This is a much easier and more accurate method than turning the red throttle dial rapidly back and forth.

With a TPC, you can operate the horn on a ProtoSound 2.0 locomotive.

Fast horn and bells

The TPC 400 also has a fast horn and bell feature. When operating MTH ProtoSound 2.0 locomotives in conventional-command mode on a TMCC layout, you need quick pulses of the horn and bell buttons to activate conventional-control ProtoSound 2.0 features, such as opening the coil couplers. It's like sending Morse code to the ProtoSound 2.0 locomotives using the horn and bell keys as dots and dashes.

Legacy CAB-2 and CAB-1 horn and bell buttons don't always produce quick-enough dots and dashes. The TPC 400 uses the 3 and 6 keys on the handheld controller to produce fast horn and bell pulses that are more acceptable to Proto-Sound 2.0 locomotives.

TPC benefits

We recommend spending the extra money for a TPC instead of a PowerMaster. You may have a small layout today, and a PowerMaster may meet your needs, but a PowerMaster does not offer the same room for growth as a TPC. Even if you do not use MTH ProtoSound-equipped locomotives, both the TPC 300 and TPC 400 offer greater power capacity and less touchy higher-amperage circuit breakers.

Advanced operation 9

Dividing a sophisticated layout into electrical blocks makes it is easier to run several trains at once.

When you were a child, you probably built a tower from basic wooden blocks, one step at a time. Sophisticated TMCC layouts are built one step at a time as well, using basic TMCC components. The bigger the tower, the more blocks. The more sophisticated the TMCC layout, the more electrical blocks and the more TMCC components.

Even a first-generation TMCC controller could handle 99 trains and dozens of accessories and track switches. That's more than adequate for even museum-sized layouts. The challenge for a sophisticated layout is managing adequate electrical power to all parts of the layout to keep those 99 trains moving.

A sophisticated layout

A sophisticated TMCC layout isn't about size as much as it is about power and number of trains, track switches, and accessories. You can build a 40-foot-long layout, but if you only operate one train at a time, your layout is large but unsophisticated.

Medium-sized and larger layouts have the track length to run three, four, or more trains at the same time, but such a layout designed as one large electrical circuit can quickly exhaust the power output of even the largest toy train transformers.

By splitting up a layout into smaller electrical blocks, you can power each block with a moderate-sized transformer.

Trains can cross from block to block without losing electrical power or TMCC control, so the result is the ability to run more locomotives at the same time. This network of power supplies can be managed by TMCC components.

Further sophistication comes with the addition of TMCC-controlled accessories and track switches and the creation of TMCC-controlled track routes.

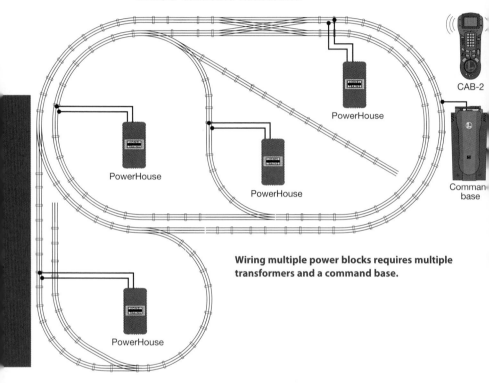

Wiring multiple power blocks requires multiple transformers and a command base.

Command control only

If you are planning a sophisticated layout that will be operated only in command-control mode, managing track power is easy. One TMCC handheld controller and command base can control the entire layout. A sophisticated command-control-only layout is divided into electrical blocks, each with a separate 18-volt power supply, all in electrical phase and sharing a common return or ground through the outside rails of the track.

Operating this layout is a snap. Just plug the transformers into a single power strip, preset the transformer handles to 18 volts (PowerHouse transformers automatically supply 18 volts), and start up your TMCC locomotive. That's it.

How big is one electrical block?

The size of an electrical block depends on how you run your trains. A block should ordinarily have no more than two or maybe three trains on it at the same time since those two or three trains all draw their power from the same transformer. Use your average train length as a rule of thumb when building blocks, and don't forget to make allowances for yards, locomotive servicing facilities, double-headed trains, and other layout features that are heavy on locomotives.

Many layouts have concentric loops of track that can be wired as individual blocks. There's no limit to the number of blocks you can build into your layout, although eventually you will reach a limit to the number of transformers under load that you can plug into a single electrical circuit of your house. If your layout grows that sophisticated, you'll need advice from an electrician.

Thinking ahead

Build your layout for the future. You may only have a single transformer and a single PowerMaster or TPC today, but your needs tomorrow may dictate additional electrical blocks and additional components.

Create electrical blocks using insulated pins in the center rails. They will be there when you need them, and for the time being, you can solder a jumper wire to connect blocks and bypass the pins. Later on, cutting a jumper wire to create an electrical block will be much easier than adding an insulated pin.

Thinking ahead also means using a wire size – 14 gauge is a good choice – that can handle future growth and additional power.

Both command and conventional control

Things get more complicated on a TMCC layout that is intended to run trains in both command control and conventional-control modes.

In conventional-control mode, trains are controlled by increasing or decreasing track voltage. To control track voltage using a CAB-1 or CAB-2 controller, you need a PowerMaster or Track Power Controller (TPC) for each electrical block.

PowerMasters and TPCs can be assigned ID numbers zero through 9, giving your handheld controller the ability to individually adjust the track voltage in 10 electrical blocks to meet the needs of up to 10 conventionally controlled trains.

You can also give some or all of the TPCs or PowerMasters the same ID number and control the voltage in an entire division

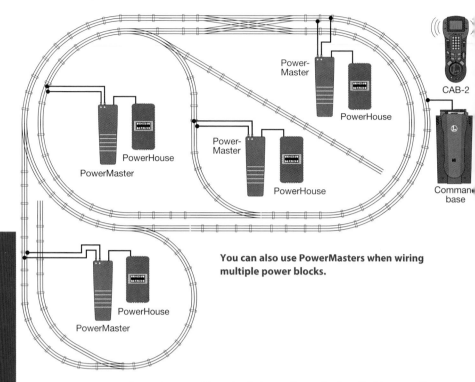

You can also use PowerMasters when wiring multiple power blocks.

of your layout with a single input from the handheld controller. Creating divisions gives you the ability to use more than 10 TPCs or PowerMasters if your layout is especially large.

Conventional control with handles

Another way to gain both command and conventional control over a multiblock layout is to use conventional transformers with throttle handles, such as Lionel's iconic postwar ZW or MTH's powerful Z-4000 (you don't have to use a Lionel transformer to power your TMCC layout).

Set all of the transformers to 18 volts for command-control operation. For conventional-control operation, simply use the transformer handles to control voltage in each transformer's block. When operating conventional-control trains in this manner without a TPC or PowerMaster, only the transformer handles can control track-block voltage, so set your TMCC controller down.

Lionel's modern ZW transformer is a hybrid. Since it already contains PowerMaster circuitry, you've got the best of both worlds. You can vary track voltage in an electrical block with the ZW's handles or with the TMCC handheld controller.

Controlling track switches

TMCC allows you to control your trains and your track, including switches, or turnouts, with a CAB-1 or CAB-2 controller.

The Aux-1 and Aux-2 buttons on a TMCC handheld controller take the place of traditional panel-mounted switch controllers. Tapping the Aux-1 key positions the selected track switch for the through route, and tapping the Aux-2 key positions the switch for the diverging route.

Each switch is assigned a number. For example, press SW on your CAB-1 or CAB-2, press key 3, and then Aux-2, and you have set switch number 3 to its diverging route.

Switches must use a power source independent of your layout's track power. To control track switches from a CAB-1 or CAB-2, you'll need a Lionel SC-2 Switch Controller or an Accessory Switch Controller (ASC). Both components are essentially electrical relays that take commands from your CAB-1 or CAB-2. (The ASC is designated good and the SC-2, better.) In addition to track switches, both components can turn two types of accessories on and off. These accessories require momentary closing of an electrical circuit to start, such as Lionel's modern-era bascule bridge, or accessories that require power to stay on, such as a rotary beacon.

SC-2 and ASC controllers

An ASC can control four switches since each switch needs three positions: straight, curved, and off. Or an ASC can turn eight accessories on and off as accessories need only two positions, on and off.

The ASC receives its signal from a TPC through a communications wire, the same wire that connects the TPC to

In conventional control, the handles on a transformer can control the voltage in a block.

An ASC can control four switches or eight accessories.

the command base. The ASC also must be connected to a transformer so its internal relays have power.

An SC-2 can control up to six switches or 12 accessories and is beefy enough to handle 20 amps through its contacts, more than you will likely ever need. It receives wireless signals from the CAB-1 or CAB-2 and comes with a wall-pack transformer to power its internal relays for accessory control. It can also use the same power that the track switches use.

The SC-2 and ASC are wired differently from one another. They are also wired differently based on whether you are activating track switches or accessories. The SC-2 is even powered differently depending on its use. Read their instruction manuals closely, or you risk damaging the TMCC components and possibly your track or accessories.

Future accessories

You can plan ahead for TMCC-controlled accessories and track switches just as you plan ahead for trackwork and wiring. Start by reading the instruction sheets for the TMCC components. Leave accessible spots on your layout for operating accessories. You may have few accessories today, but you will likely add more in the future.

If you have accessories today, but aren't ready for ASC or SC-2 components, group your controllers in one location, ideally near a power supply. When you are ready to add TMCC controllers, the wiring will already be in place, and TMCC installation will be a simple swap-out instead of a layout rewiring job.

Versatile products

The SC-2 and ASC aren't limited to track switches and traditional Lionel-style accessories. Anything on your layout

SC-2 accessory applications

Here is a partial list of Lionel postwar and modern accessories that can be activated using the SC-2. Specific instructions to wire these accessories are in Lionel's SC-2 instruction booklet. Other accessories (from Lionel or other manufacturers) can be wired similarly.

Rotary Beacon (nos. 394, 494, 6-12831)

Control Tower (nos. 192, 6-12878)

Floodlight Tower (nos. 195, 395, 6-12759, 6-12886)

Icing Station (nos. 352, 6-12847)

Water Tower (nos. 30, 138)

Lumber Mill (nos. 464, 6-12873)

Switch Tower (no. 445)

Diesel Fueling Station (nos. 415, 6-12877)

Oil Derrick (nos. 445, 6-12902)

Lumber Loader (no. 364)

Coal Tower (nos. 97, 6-32921)

Freight Station (no. 356)

Whistle or Diesel Horn Shack (nos. 125, 6-12737, 6-12903)

Aircraft Pylon (no. 6-32920 and similar)

Bascule Bridge (no. 6-12948)

Oil Drum Loader (no. 6-22997)

Uncoupling Track (nos. 6-65149, 6-12840)

that gets turned on and off, such as lighting and sound effect devices, can be linked to an ASC or an SC-2 and controlled with the CAB-1 or CAB-2 in your hand.

The relays inside the SC-2 and ASC can throw other relays with appropriate contacts capable of handling all sorts of electrical devices. If you wanted, you could use your hand-held controller to activate a relay that starts up your television or triggers your electric garage-door opener.

Programming routes

You can use your CAB-1 or CAB-2 to create routes. Setting a series of track switches to create a specific path for a train is called a route.

Picture your locomotive following a switch off the main line through a series of four yard-track switches to a final switch leading to an engine-servicing area. Instead of setting all six switches individually, a CAB-1 or CAB-2 controller can record the switch settings for a given route. Later playback of the route sends your locomotive all the way to the servicing track by pressing only the RTE button and the appropriate route number on the keypad.

The newer Legacy CAB-2 has a vastly expanded route function accessed by the Record button – it can record and store roughly 1,000 commands, with a maximum delay of up to 400 seconds between events. It will save and play back any function that can be controlled by a CAB-2.

To create a recording with a CAB-2, press and hold the Record button for five seconds and release. Operate the CAB-2 as you normally would. The system will remember everything you do until you tap the Record button again. To save the recorded sequence, press and hold the Record button for five seconds.

Controlling layout accessories

Back in the heyday of toy train accessories, who'd have thought they could be controlled by digital commands? But using TMCC components such as the SC-2, ASC, Accessory Motor Controller (AMC), Operating Track Controller (OTC), and Accessory Voltage Controller (AVC), you can do just that.

The SC-2 and ASC can trigger accessories you would otherwise activate through a push button (either momentary contact or hold-down) or an On/Off switch. You can use multiple ASCs or SC-2s on your layout, all programmed to respond to different keypad numbers, depending on your needs.

Motor-controlled and other accessories

The CAB-1 and CAB-2 controllers really shine when operating motor-controlled accessories such as Lionel's no. 164 log loader, no. 464 sawmill, or various gantry cranes. Using an AMC component on your TMCC layout allows the red dial on your CAB-1 or CAB-2 to control the speed of the accessory's motor, or in the case of accessories like the gantry crane, the left-right rotation of its swing.

The handheld controller's dial and keypad take the place of the buttons, levers, and dials of the accessory's original hard-wired controller.

Look for Lionel to offer more and more of its accessories in command and conventional versions. Conventional versions can be operated by TMCC, but you'll need an SC-2, ASC, or other TMCC component. Command versions, while pricier, already contain a TMCC receiver and control mechanism within the accessory.

Two other handy accessory-related TMCC components are the Operating Track Controller and Accessory Voltage Controller. The OTC can control two operating tracks or four uncoupling track sections. Its controls are momentary contact only, so unless you fall asleep with your finger on the button, there's no way you can burn out the controller or the track section.

The AVC offers the ability to customize the voltage sent to a specific accessory since many postwar accessories respond best to different voltages. The AVC's role is similar to variable voltage posts on postwar transformers that offered 8, 10, 12, or 14 volts.

Lash-ups and sophisticated train control

Locomotive control can also be more sophisticated. TMCC offers the ability to create lash-ups, where multiple powered locomotives respond as a single command-controlled unit. It also has the ability to set locomotive momentum and stall rates, and with TMCC, you can even set a maximum speed to curb overly enthusiastic operators.

Any TMCC-equipped locomotive can be coupled to another TMCC-equipped locomotive in a lash-up controlled as a unit by your CAB-1 or CAB-2. You can even lash up three or more locomotives in forward- or reverse-facing directions. Lash-ups operate as a unit, addressed by the TR button instead of the ENG button.

Similar in design to a TPC, the AVC regulates voltage to accessories.

Realistically, however, like-motored locomotives make for better lash-up partners. Locomotives with Pullmor motors have different speed and acceleration characteristics than those with can-style motors. If mixed, your lash-up partners may cooperate, or one could either drag or push its partner around the track.

Momentum and stall speed

Real trains are immensely heavy and take considerable time to pick up speed or slow down. To model this effect, the TMCC CAB-1 offers three levels of momentum control, accessed by the L, M, and H buttons at the bottom of the controller. You have more settings to choose from using a Legacy CAB-2. For example, pressing and holding M opens a display on the

LCD screen that allows you to select from eight levels of medium momentum.

Stall speed lets you set the starting speed of each locomotive, keeping you from spinning the red dial a half-turn or more before seeing any response from a given engine. For locomotives that support this function, press Set at the base of the CAB-1 or CAB-2, start the engine rolling, and then slowly turn the throttle dial counter-clockwise until the locomotive stops. Press Set a second time and the system will remember the stall power level for that locomotive. This is particularly useful when lashing up TMCC-equipped locomotives having Pullmor motors with locomotives that have can motors.

Other control odds and ends

Three other advanced-level TMCC control features are transitional control, sticky keys, and the Action Recorder Controller (ARC).

Transitional control. In a way, transitional control is cheating. It allows you to operate one conventional-control locomotive and one or more command-control locomotives on the same track at the same time.

Command-controlled locomotives are designed to operate best at 18 volts, but many can operate at 15, 12, or even 10 volts. Acceleration, pulling ability, and top speed, however, will suffer as the voltage drops. A conventional-controlled locomotive at 18 volts might be launched off the table and onto to the floor, but the same locomotive might easily stay on the track at 12 volts.

If your layout were only given 12 volts of electricity, you could keep the conventional-controlled locomotive on the track yet also operate a command-controlled locomotive at the same time. That's transitional control.

Transitional control is most easily accomplished if your layout is powered by a traditional transformer with handles. Simply set the throttle to the proper voltage for the conventional-control locomotive and then fire up the command-controlled locomotive with your CAB-1 or CAB-2. You can also accomplish the same thing with a PowerHouse transformer. Power up your layout in conventional-control mode to get your conventional-controlled locomotive operating at the desired speed and then start the command-controlled locomotive.

In theory, transitional control works great, but in reality it is a compromise. You'll need to constantly fiddle with the track voltage to keep a conventional-controlled locomotive operating around curves and up and down grades, and each change in track voltage will also affect the performance of the command-controlled locomotive.

Sticky keys remember recently used commands.

Sticky keys. Sticky keys aren't adhesive. Instead, they remember your most recent command inputs. If you press ENG and the keypad numbers 6 and 7, the horn, bell, coupler, tower talk, and all of the other features associated with locomotive 67 can be accessed by pressing the keys ENG and 6 and 7 over and over again. All of the top-row keys – SW, ACC, RTE, TR, and ENG – are sticky.

The action recorder. The functions of the action recorder are built into the Legacy CAB-2. For users of CAB-1, the ARC component remembers everything. It records your series of CAB-1 keystrokes and throttle inputs for playback at a later time.

Where to start?

With so many choices for more advanced TMCC operators, it's hard to know where to start. But just as a child playing with building blocks, you take things one step at a time.

First, learn about TMCC concepts and components by reading magazine articles and books, by talking to fellow hobbyists at a club or a train shop, and by looking for information on manufacturer and enthusiast Web sites (see page 62). Many manufacturer's Web sites today offer free downloadable versions of their instruction manuals.

Next, decide which features are right for you and fit within your technical comfort zone (not all of us are electrical engineers!). Make a list. Then ask yourself how you like to operate trains. Switching? Changing routes? Just sitting back and watching? Match your operating habits to your list.

Finally, ask around and visit some layouts operated with TMCC. Hands-on experience is the best teacher.

10 Converting locomotives

Any locomotive can be converted to TMCC. Whatever the era or manufacturer, today, all locomotives can be converted to TrainMaster Command Control. Companies such as Digital Dynamics and The Electric RR Co. offer TMCC components that you can install in an existing non-command-controlled locomotive to covert it to command control.

A converted locomotive can do anything a new Lionel TMCC-equipped locomotive can do, depending on the features of the conversion circuitry and those the locomotive originally came with, such as smoke, special lighting, and a sound system.

Converting a locomotive to TMCC is also a prime opportunity to add sound, additional lighting, a smoke generator, and perhaps even cruise control to a locomotive. Different TMCC circuit boards can accommodate those features, and you can control all these add-ons through a CAB-1 or CAB-2 controller. Just imagine your childhood Lionel steamer chugging down your layout today, complete with RailSounds and a puffing smoke generator.

Being comfortable and creative

Some conversions are a snap to accomplish, and others are a challenge. You will need to be comfortable handling circuit boards and miniature plugs and jacks. For older locomotive conversions, you'll need to solder a few wires.

You'll also need to be creative. Since hundreds of locomotives are potential conversion candidates, there are no instructions for any specific locomotive. Installation instructions cover MTH ProtoSound-equipped locomotive conversions, prewar and postwar AC-motored locomotive conversions, and modern DC-motored locomotive conversions. (These locomotives use rectifiers to convert AC track power to operate DC can-style motors.)

Some locomotives have more space inside their body shells to accommodate TMCC circuit boards than others. Also, conversion circuit boards can come in various sizes to accommodate different features and needs. If your conversion locomotive is a postwar diesel with a horn, it has different needs than a brass steam locomotive already equipped with a sound system and a smoke generator.

Diesel locomotives are generally good conversion candidates. There is often plenty of space for circuit boards between the truck-mounted motors. Diesel shells are almost always made of plastic, so there is little concern that a conversion circuit board will be damaged by an electrical short if it touches the inside surface of the shell. Also, the underside of the plastic roof is a good spot for the TMCC antenna.

Steam locomotives are tougher conversion candidates. Circuit boards are rectangular in shape, while steam locomotive boilers are cylindrical. Worse, the boilers are usually crammed with a motor, a smoke generator, and a drive shaft or spur gears. That leaves only the space inside the tender for a TMCC circuit board, which necessitates a wire harness and plug and jack to connect the circuit board to the locomotive's motor and track power pickups.

The die-cast metal tender shells found on many modern steam locomotives create further installation and antenna placement challenges.

Sound and smoke

Steam locomotives also present an audio challenge. While diesel engine sounds – revving up or revving down – can be controlled by motor speed, a steam locomotive's chuff sound must be in synchronization with the rotation of its drivers and the puffing of its smokestack. Voltage or motor speed regulation won't work in a steady 18-volt command-control environment.

Locomotives that never had anything more than a whistle usually require installation of an audio timing system. To regulate the chuffing sound and the puffing smoke, a small reed switch is mounted next to a wheel of the locomotive, and a magnet on the inside of the wheel turns the switch on and off.

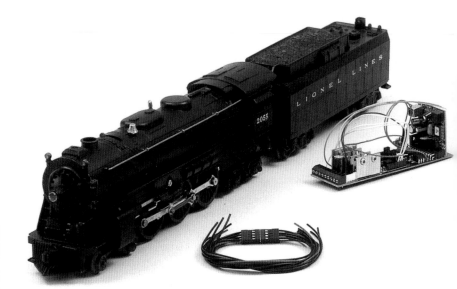

MTH locomotive conversions

Early ProtoSound locomotives from MTH Electric Trains
are among the most popular TMCC conversions. Conversion supply companies have specific circuit boards that allow
you to use the original MTH locomotive sounds in a TMCC
environment. Some conversions require additional wiring
for smoke generators and lighting, while other conversions
amount to little more than pulling off one circuit board, pushing on another, and plugging in an antenna.

Prewar and postwar conversions

Postwar Lionel diesels and steam engines and even prewar
locomotives are also frequently converted locomotives. These
conversions employ circuit boards specially designed for postwar
and prewar open-frame AC motors. Since there were no circuit
boards when these locomotives were originally produced, you'll
need to give some thought to the positioning of the TMCC
circuit board, and you'll also have to solder several connections.

For a steam locomotive conversion, you'll require an additional electrical tether wire, a plug, and a jack to connect the circuit board in the tender to the motor inside the boiler shell.

In addition, you can add Lionel's RailSounds to your postwar locomotives. The RailSounds circuit board plugs into a TMCC circuit board, and you'll have to find a home inside your locomotive for a speaker.

Conversions aren't limited to O gauge locomotives. American Flyer S gauge locomotives and Standard gauge locomotives can also be converted to TMCC.

You may need to place circuit boards in the tender when converting a steam locomotive to TMCC.

Conversion suppliers

The two chief suppliers of conversion components are The Electric RR Co. and Digital Dynamics. Both offer conversion circuit boards for different applications – everything from postwar locomotives with a whistle or horn to early MTH ProtoSound locomotives.

Conversion components range from about $80 for basic motor control to $200 or more for fully featured TMCC circuitry including Lionel RailSounds.

Even if you are not in the market for a locomotive conversion, suppliers offer other TMCC-operated enhancements, such as smoke generators, circuits for Lionel operating cars (you can activate an operating milk car anywhere on a layout), and add-on lighting packages.

11 Additional answers

The TMCC operator's manual describes the basics of TMCC. But there is always more to learn, and that's especially true with the more robust TMCC feature set introduced by Lionel's second-generation Legacy system. But there will always be specific questions that don't have definitive answers because no two O gauge layouts are exactly alike.

There are dozens of function-related troubleshooting tips throughout the TMCC instructions and in the booklets packaged with various TMCC components. They address the most common problems you may encounter with your TMCC system. Repeating them here would be, well, repetitious. Instead, here are some answers you may not find in the manuals.

Does a Lionel TMCC-equipped locomotive operate better on a TMCC layout than one from another manufacturer?
The TMCC circuitry in non-Lionel brands works just as well as the circuitry in a Lionel locomotive. Depending on locomotive models, it may perform identically to that of a comparable Lionel engine. Lionel's new-generation Legacy system has not yet been made available to non-Lionel manufacturers. Lionel Legacy locomotives operated by Legacy CAB-2 command control offer better performance and an enhanced set of features when compared to the original-generation TMCC circuit boards found in non-Lionel locomotives.

Is there an inexpensive way to convert non-TMCC locomotives to TMCC?

Using components from companies like The Electric RR Co. or Digital Dynamics is the only way to go. Depending on the locomotive and its features, expect to pay around $100 for a basic conversion board.

What is a command-ready locomotive?

It's a lower-priced Lionel locomotive designed to be upgraded to command control at a later time. The locomotive comes with a socket that accepts a TMCC circuit board but not the board itself.

What is the difference between command-controlled versions of modern Lionel accessories and regular versions?

Command-controlled accessories have built-in TMCC receivers.

What is a command-equipped operating car?

It, too, has a built-in TMCC receiver and is assigned an address as if it were a locomotive. Command-equipped cars offer RailSounds effects and other special effects accessible through the CAB-1 or CAB-2 keypads.

Can more than one CAB-1 or CAB-2 controller be used at the same time when there is more than one operator?

Definitely yes, and sly operators can even steal trains from their co-operators. At train shows, some modular clubs change the crystals in their CAB-1s, or change the frequency of their CAB-2s using the frequency selector switch on the underside of the command base, to avoid interfering with a neighboring TMCC-controlled modular layout.

Why do some TMCC-equipped locomotives speed up unexpectedly when going through metal bridges or wire-screen tunnels?

They are losing a clear signal because of the metal framework of the bridge or tunnel. If you encounter this problem on your layout, run a wire from the bridge to an earth ground, a water pipe or similar source, not the transformer's ground wire. There have been isolated instances where metal components such as beams in the walls or ceiling of a basement or train room cause interference.

Will a cordless phone or CB radio interfere with TMCC signals?

Although the CAB-1 uses a CB bandwidth to transmit commands, interference from a nearby radio transmitter is unlikely. The CAB-2 uses the same frequency as a cordless phone, but again, interference is unlikely. If you do encounter problems with a CAB-2 signal, try changing the command base frequency.

If a Lionel locomotive features command-control circuitry, and an MTH ProtoSound 2.0 locomotive features command-control circuitry, will the MTH locomotive work on a TMCC layout?

Only in conventional-control mode. The ProtoSound 2.0 locomotive doesn't have the same type of receiver as a TMCC-equipped locomotive, so it will never receive a TMCC signal.

Does TMCC require the use of Lionel tubular track?

No. But since non-tubular track does not have metal ties connecting the two outside rails, make sure the signal wire from the command base is connected to both outside rails, or an insulated outside rail on your layout could create a signal gap.

Where to get more information

Besides hands-on information from hobby shops, fellow operators, and O gauge railroad clubs, you can also find TMCC information in Lionel catalogs and in the pages of *Classic Toy Trains* magazine or on ClassicToyTrains.com. Here are other Web sites that offer TMCC information:

Lionel.com – Lionel's Web site includes a wealth of TMCC information and products.

Coilcouplers.com – There's nothing to buy here, but it's the first site you should go to if you're new to TMCC. Be sure to check out the interactive tutorials.

Electricrr.com – The Electric RR Co. makes TMCC components to convert non-command-controlled locomotives to TMCC. It also offers kits for operating cars.

Digitdynam.com – Digital Dynamics offers TMCC conversion components.

Ogaugerr.com – Click on Forum and navigate to the discussion area specifically devoted to TMCC.

DCS components 12

DCS has only two basic components: a handheld controller and a Track Interface Unit.

In the late 1990s, MTH was busy developing its original conventional-control-only ProtoSound trains. By 2002, MTH was ready for the next step: ProtoSound 2.0 locomotives that could be run in conventional-control mode or in command-control mode using MTH's Digital Command System.

In the broadest sense, DCS does the same thing that TMCC does – allows you to independently operate more than one locomotive on the same track at the same time. How DCS does this is very different from TMCC.

DCS controller

DCS uses only two basic components: a controller and a base unit. Power is supplied by an outside source, such as an MTH Z-4000 transformer or another toy train transformer.

Like Lionel's TMCC, DCS offers you a handheld cordless controller to operate trains, track, and accessories. Unlike the CAB-1 or CAB-2, the DCS controller doesn't have a specific name, so we'll just call it the DCS controller.

If you own a cell phone, take it out of your pocket, walk over to your living room, and place your cell phone next to your television remote control. That's a fair comparison of the

advancement and complexity of the DCS controller over Lionel's first-generation CAB-1. The DCS manual is 120 pages long while Lionel's original TMCC manual was 48 pages.

Like a cellular telephone, DCS is menu-driven and uses a small LCD screen to show menu selections. Select from one of its main menus – sound, control, system, and advanced – and you can move through layers of menus to find the feature you seek.

Buttons and keypad controls

The DCS controller has 31 buttons and a thumbwheel. That sounds like a lot, but DCS does a lot. The buttons are logically arranged, and their positions and functions follow the pattern introduced by the CAB-1. The 8" x 3" controller fits comfortably in your hand and is powered by four AAA batteries.

Auxiliary (AUX), accessory (ACC), switch (SW), and track (TR) buttons are arranged in an arc around the thumbwheel. Another arc features bell (BELL), engine (ENG), and whistle/horn (W/H) control buttons. Located beneath the thumbwheel, the menu and direction (DIR) buttons complete a circle around the thumbwheel. The primary buttons for locomotive operation – bell, engine, whistle/horn, and direction – are the closest to the thumbwheel and molded in different colors.

On the bottom half of the DCS controller is a numeric keypad with functions similar to those of the TMCC keypad: sound volume, start up and shut down, headlights, and smoke. One button on the numeric keypad is sub-labeled ProtoCast for playing music from a cassette or CD player through the locomotive's ProtoSound 2.0 speaker. Another, sub-labeled PFA, kicks off the passenger or freight train announcement/ sound effects sequence.

A red E-Stop button for emergency stops and a Read button are located at the very bottom of the controller. At the top of the controller, the B/L button turns on the LCD screen's backlight, and the MIC button allows you to broadcast your voice through the locomotive's speaker. (There's a small microphone inside the top of the DCS controller.)

Rolling the thumbwheel

The DCS controller's thumbwheel does double duty. You use it as the throttle as well as scrolling through the menus listed on the LCD screen. By pressing down on the thumbwheel,

With 31 buttons and a thumbwheel, the DCS controller does a lot.

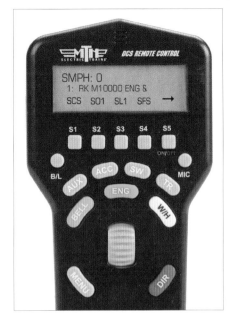

The function of the soft keys, labeled S1 through S5, corresponds to the matching code at the bottom of the controller screen.

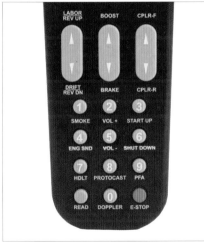

The numeric keypad controls volume, headlights, smoke, and other functions.

you select the menu, just like clicking the mouse of a home computer.

The thumbwheel has no Start or Stop positions. Similar to the red dial on Lionel's handheld controller, the thumbwheel spins continuously, allowing you to jump between locomotives operating at different speeds without getting caught at the wrong setting. However, the DCS controller's thumbwheel has clearly defined notches, or clicks, but there are no start or stop notches.

Five soft keys

Along the bottom of the DCS controller's screen are five soft keys labeled S1 through S5. They are soft in function, not in touch. Their functions vary with the menu selected on the LCD screen. Selections listed on the menu line up with each of the five keys. Those selections become the labels for the soft keys until a different menu is chosen.

Signal and power management

The DCS controller sends 900-megahertz signals to the Track Interface Unit (TIU). If 900 megahertz sounds familiar, it's the same bandwidth used by cordless telephones and the TMCC CAB-2.

The TIU is a 6" x 10" box with banana-plug jacks running down its two long sides. It has several other input and output jacks of various designs along its short sides.

The DCS controller and the TIU live on a two-way street. Information is passed from the controller to the TIU and then to locomotives. In return, the TIU gives the DCS controller feedback on the status of locomotives, track, and accessories.

The DCS controller can also speak to the TIU through a telephone handset cord. It's a useful tool when trouble-shooting DCS-signal interference. The cord needs to be a telephone handset cord, not the line cord. The controller and TIU each have handset cord jacks.

Managing the DCS signal

The TIU receives a signal from the DCS controller, processes the information, and sends an appropriate signal through the track rails into each ProtoSound 2.0 locomotive. Piggybacking the signal onto the electrical power to the rails is a major difference between DCS and TMCC, in which signal and track power are independent.

The DCS signal passes from the TIU through a layout's wiring, through the center rail of the track, and through the locomotive pickup rollers to the ProtoSound 2.0 signal receiver inside the locomotive. The signal completes its circuit back out of the locomotive, through the outside rails, through the layout's wiring, and back to the TIU.

With such a roundabout route, clean track, clean locomotives, and reliable electrical connections are key to a fully functioning DCS layout.

Managing track power

Track power from a separate transformer feeds into one side of the TIU, picks up the DCS signal, and leaves the other side of the TIU for the track.

The TIU has four track feeds, or ports. One side of the TIU has four input ports and the other side has four output ports. The two innermost ports are fixed-voltage ports. If 18 volts go into one of these two ports, 18 volts come out. If 9 volts go in, 9 volts come out. Voltage of these two ports is controlled by the transformer powering your layout and cannot be regulated by the DCS controller. These fixed-voltage ports are suggested for command-control mode only.

The two track ports on the outer ends of the TIU are variable-voltage ports, and they are controlled by the DCS controller. If 18 volts go in, nothing comes out until the DCS controller addresses the port or track and the voltage is turned up using the thumbwheel. These two ports can operate in both conventional-control and command-control modes. In conventional-control mode, the thumbwheel on the DCS controller is the throttle, which adjusts track voltage as needed. The DIR, BELL, and W/H keys function the same as those on a conventional transformer. In command-control operation, you can use the DCS controller's thumbwheel to set the track to 18 volts and then begin command-control operation.

To operate conventional-controlled locomotives, DCS, unlike TMCC, doesn't need an additional component similar to a PowerMaster or TPC.

The TIU has four power ports, In on one side, and Out on the other.

Powering a TIU

You should power the TIU from a separate source. The TIU needs a small amount of internal power to operate. It can get this power from your track transformer plugged into fixed-voltage port 1. If you are only using a variable-voltage port, you'll need to use jumper wires to connect the hot and common terminals of the variable port to fixed port number 1. Otherwise, the TIU won't have any power to operate its internal circuits.

But you can power the TIU independently from the track transformer. One of the short sides of the TIU contains a jack marked Auxiliary Power. The barrel-style plugs from transformers such as MTH's Z-750 and Lionel starter sets fit perfectly. You can also use a small, wall-plug-style transformer as long as its output is between 12 and 24 volts AC and 1 to 10 amps.

The Z-4000 transformer is ideal for DCS use.

Z-4000 and other transformers

MTH designed DCS with its 400-watt Z-4000 transformer in mind, but you can use any AC transformer capable of sustaining 18 volts and having adequate circuit-breaker protection.

If you want to use a Lionel postwar transformer, you'll need to install a fuse between the transformer and the TIU. Postwar transformers don't have fast enough circuit breakers to adequately protect TIU circuits. You'll need a heavy-duty in-line fuse holder (Radio Shack part no. 270-1217 for example). With it, use a 15-amp fast-acting fuse (Radio Shack no. 270-1040 or an equivalent).

DCS buyer's guide

Here's a list of MTH's DCS components and their part numbers:

- DCS Remote Control System (50-1001): handheld controller (50-1002) and Track Interface Unit (50-1003)

- Accessory Interface Unit (50-1004)

ProtoSound 2.0 locomotives **13**

In early 2000, MTH began selling ProtoSound 2.0-equipped locomotives, and today, all locomotives produced by MTH are equipped with ProtoSound 2.0. Evolved from MTH's original ProtoSound locomotives, the 2.0 locomotives contain new sound systems with far more options, cruise control, and a DCS signal receiver.

ProtoSound 2.0-equipped locomotives are the only locomotives that have DCS receivers. At present, MTH does not let other manufacturers use DCS receivers in their locomotives. MTH also does not license any independent electronics companies to produce DCS receivers for installation in postwar and other locomotives.

MTH has produced ProtoSound 2.0 upgrade boards for original ProtoSound locomotives and some non-MTH steam and diesel locomotives. The company encourages owners to have the work done at an MTH Authorized Service Center, since the upgrade will involve significant rewiring, new mounting brackets, and soldering.

Original ProtoSound locomotives can operate on layouts equipped with DCS in conventional-control mode only. They don't have DCS receivers, and they don't have any sockets or similar devices to accept installation of a DCS receiver.

Only ProtoSound 2.0 locomotives can operate in DCS command-control mode.

Command or conventional operation

All ProtoSound 2.0 locomotives can be operated in command-control mode or conventional-control mode. A ProtoSound 2.0 locomotive does not have an external switch, so it selects a mode by sensing the DCS signal. If the locomotive's circuitry senses a DCS signal on start-up, it will operate in command-control mode. If there is no DCS signal, the locomotive starts up in conventional-control mode, moving as the track voltage dictates and following the traditional forward-neutral-reverse cycle of changing direction.

That long, long list of features

The DCS controller can activate more than 60 ProtoSound 2.0 locomotive features in command-control mode. And if that's not enough, MTH says that DCS is designed to accommodate as many as 100 features activated by soft key menus.

Some basic features, like horn/whistle, bell, couplers, and passenger station or freight yard sounds can be activated in conventional-control mode without a DCS controller.

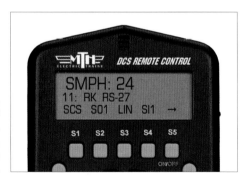

DCS tells you the running speed of ProtoSound 2.0 locomotives in scale miles per hour.

Scale miles per hour

In command-control mode, you can operate ProtoSound 2.0-equipped locomotives in scale miles per hour. Each click of the thumbwheel is one scale mph increment, and your speed is shown on the DCS controller's screen. No command-control system has done this before, and this effect, more than any other DCS feature, gives you the sensation that you are operating your locomotive, not just electrically manipulating the track it is riding upon.

Variable features

Each ProtoSound 2.0 locomotive has a slightly different menu of features, depending on whether it is steam, diesel, or electric; whether it has a smoke unit; what types of lighting it has; and its pricing. The Premier line of locomotives offer more features than locomotives in the RailKing line.

But even the less expensive RailKing diesels and steam locomotives have plenty of features. They include start-up and shut-down sounds; independent volume control of horn or whistle, bell, and engine noise; cab chatter; squeaking brakes; track clickety clack; extra idle and in-motion sounds; and a Doppler sound effect.

Steam locomotives have chuff and smoke volume control, and if equipped, firebox glow control. Diesel locomotives offer control over engine rpm sounds and control over modern features such as ditch lights.

Other nonaudio features include elapsed time, running time, track measurement, cruise control, and even a locomotive maintenance reminder.

The list seems endless, and it can't help but satisfy even the most demanding command-control operator.

Starter RailKing locomotives offer many DCS features.

Only the features of a locomotive show up in a menu.

Feature menus

All of the ProtoSound 2.0 features are accessed through the menus on the DCS controller. You can access the most often-used features by using the numeric keys on the controller and a few adjacent buttons. You can use the soft keys at the top of the controller and the thumbwheel to get to other features listed in submenus.

With so many features, it can be confusing, so it is helpful that only the features for a specific locomotive show up in its menus. If you are operating a diesel locomotive that is not equipped with ditch lights, there won't be a menu selection for ditch lights.

You also have the ability to change the order of the features in a specific menu, so you can put the ones you use the most often at the top of the list.

The soft-key menu choices are all given in three-letter codes. If you can't remember the codes, you can go to the scroll-down menu, which spells out the abbreviations.

Putting DCS on your layout **14**

DCS can be installed on a layout of any size, from a basic 4 x 8-foot tabletop layout to one that would fill a six-car garage.

DCS operates on layouts of any size.

DCS layouts have the same basic needs as Lionel TMCC layouts. They need wiring that can handle 18 continuous volts, rolling stock with lights that won't burn out at 18 volts, and electrical power blocks on bigger layouts where a single transformer would be inadequate. (For a rundown on electrical blocks and power needs, flip back to chapter 5.)

DCS communication signals are piggybacked through the very same wires that carry electricity to your track and back to the transformer. Because of that, the key to a successful DCS layout has less to do with its size and more to do with the way it is wired.

If you encounter DCS signal problems on your layout, you can make some basic wiring changes to boost the strength of your signal.

Traditional wiring

Traditional O gauge layout wiring schemes use a bus system to transport electricity to the track. By running a power wire and a common wire from the two transformer terminals down the length of your layout, you create bus wires.

Wires connected to the outer and center rails of the track tap into the bus wires like branches on a tree, and all sections of the layout – even those farthest away from the transformer – receive adequate electricity.

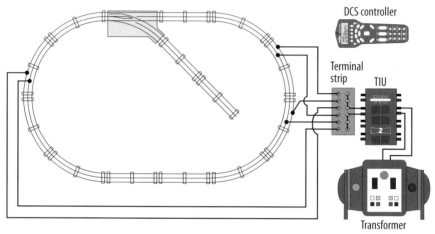

DCS controller

Terminal strip

TIU

Transformer

Star wiring

Electricity doesn't care if the wire from your transformer to your center rail is 5 feet long and the return wire from your outside rail is 15 feet long with three additional wires that split off to trackside accessories.

DCS, however, does care. The DCS signal is strongest when its path to your center rail and the path back from your outer rail are about the same distance and have no diversions.

That's why MTH recommends star wiring on DCS layouts. Instead of a wiring system that looks like branches of a tree, star wiring radiates from a central point and looks like, well, a star.

DCS will work on many layouts without star wiring, but how well its signal travels back and forth on layouts without star wiring depends on how your layout is wired. But you won't know until you try it.

How star wiring works

On a star-wired layout, paired wires (power and common) go to terminal blocks and then radiate to all points of the layout that need electricity. MTH recommends using speaker wire or lamp cord because these wires are already paired.

And since the wires are paired, the distance electricity travels to reach the track and the distance it travels to return are equal and without diversions.

Understanding DCS

DCS is a sophisticated animal. If you are comfortable with personal computers and cellular telephones, you'll be at home with DCS.

Before taking the plunge, examine your layout with a critical eye. Is your wiring done right, or is it a mishmash of undersized connections twisted together and covered with electrical tape? With DCS, it will make a difference.

Once you've purchased DCS, read the manual and watch MTH's instructional video that is included with each DCS set.

Finally, be patient. It takes time for the DCS system to communicate back and forth.

Wiring DCS doesn't like

Since the DCS signal is strongest using paired wires of equal length, here are some common layout wiring techniques that may cause problems. Remember that the DCS signal is more sensitive to wiring connections than is the flow of electricity.

Common ground wiring. Technically, the return wire to the transformer isn't a ground wire (but we'll save that discussion for electrical engineers).

Using common return wiring sets up a crazy path for the DCS signal to return from a locomotive's ProtoSound 2.0 circuit board to the Track Interface Unit (TIU).

Think of the signal as water and trace its flow from the track back to your TIU. The more twists, turns, and diversions the return flow makes, the more the return signal deteriorates.

Ultimately, with such a zig-zag route, the signal deteriorates on some sections of track to a point where your DCS controller will not recognize the ProtoSound 2.0 locomotive on the track.

Toggle switches. You may have numerous toggle switches on your layout that control power to insulated sidings or other stretches of track. Usually the toggle switch is cut into the wire going to the center rail of the track.

While these switches may work great in conventional-control mode, you've created a situation where the wires running to and from a siding are of unequal length. You're also asking the incoming DCS signal to run through the contact points of a toggle switch.

Relay-controlled blocks. On a conventional-control layout, relay-controlled blocks allow you to operate more than one locomotive at the same time by keeping trailing trains from rear-ending those ahead. With DCS, the signal must

Strengthening signals

Achieving good signal strength can be frustrating for owners of sophisticated layouts. Here are three tips to follow if you are having trouble with signal strength.

If you are struggling to add your first ProtoSound 2.0 locomotive to the controller's roster, follow the advice in the DCS user's manual. Place the locomotive on a length of test track separate from your layout and then load the locomotive's information into your DCS components.

Use the signal-strength feature of ProtoSound 2.0 locomotives to identify areas of your layout that are not receiving strong signals. Signal strength should be at least 7, but you can get by with less. Get several sets of good alligator-clip test wires. Go section by section and connect the TIU output-port posts directly to the troublesome track to see if signal strength improves. Then, one by one, reintroduce the regular electrical components used on that section of your layout to the circuit. These steps are the same as when troubleshooting an electrical short. Possible trouble spots include toggle-switch-controlled sections of track, relay-controlled sections of track, and track that shares a common return or ground line with other parts of your layout, including accessories.

Add light bulbs to your layout. Really. Attaching an 18-volt light bulb across the output-port terminals of the TIU or across the power and return wires at low-signal areas of layouts can dramatically improve signal strength. Without getting too technical, the improvement occurs because the power draw of the light bulb cleans up signals reflected back into the TIU from the track. This technique is detailed on MTH's Web site.

pass through the relay wiring, facing the same challenges as in toggle-switch wiring.

Hooking up DCS components

While signal-strength issues are complex, setting up your DCS components is quite easy. To operate ProtoSound 2.0 locomotives in command-control mode, you need the DCS controller, a TIU, and a transformer. You don't need any extra components to operate DCS in conventional-control mode.

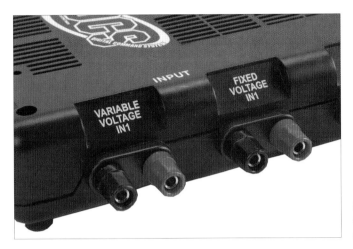

Using fixed port 1
supplies the TIU
with power.

Plugging in your TIU

The TIU needs at least two connections, one being input
from the transformer and the other output to the track.

You have several connection choices: fixed-voltage input
and output ports 1 and 2 or variable-voltage input and output
ports 1 and 2. Fixed-voltage terminals are used for command-
only operation. Whatever voltage your transformer sends to
the TIU is the voltage that is sent to the track. The DCS controller will not be able to alter the voltage in the fixed ports.

Variable-voltage ports allow you to operate both command-
control locomotives and conventional-control locomotives. The
DCS controller can alter the voltage leaving the variable ports
and heading to the track.

Power for the TIU

The TIU needs a little bit of power itself to operate. If it does
not have power, commands from your DCS controller will not
be received (and a red LED on top of the TIU will not glow).
Using fixed port number 1 automatically supplies the TIU
with power (see pages 67-68).

15 Operating DCS locomotives

A ProtoSound 2.0 locomotive knows its name and features. DCS is unlike any other O gauge model railroading experience. The parallels with Lionel's TMCC go only so far. The DCS controller, Track Interface Unit (TIU), and the Proto-Sound 2.0 locomotives are all interactive players on your layout, communicating by digital code back and forth to one another.

Turn on your layout

Once your TIU and transformer are hooked up to your layout, you're ready to begin DCS operation. With the track power off, place a ProtoSound 2.0 locomotive on the track. Power up your layout to 18 volts and make sure the red LED inside the TIU is glowing. Turn on the DCS controller using soft key number 5 (marked On/Off). Since there are four track input ports from the TIU, make sure the controller is addressing the proper track using the TR button. Then follow the menus on the DCS controller's screen.

Your locomotive won't go anywhere yet. The DCS signal is on the track, so the locomotive automatically is in command-control mode, but it's awaiting a wake-up call from your DCS controller.

Smart locomotives

ProtoSound 2.0 locomotives are unlike any other O gauge locomotives – each one knows its name and its features. The circuitry in each locomotive is imprinted with the locomotive's name, a list of sound and lighting features specific to the locomotive, and even the locomotive's cumulative running time and scale mileage.

All of this locomotive information is shared with the DCS controller when you introduce the locomotive to your layout. The locomotive's name, assigned numeric ID address, and list of features are then stored in your DCS components.

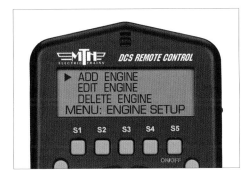

The DCS controller guides you through the process of adding an engine.

Addressing locomotives

With your locomotive on the track for the first time, press the gray Menu button, scroll down to System with the thumbwheel, select System by pressing inward on the thumbwheel, and then follow the menus to select Engine Setup, Add Engine, and Add MTH Engine.

DCS takes over from here as you sit back and watch. The controller's screen will show "Looking for Engine" for about 15 seconds. While you are waiting, the DCS controller, TIU, and locomotive are communicating, and the locomotive's name and feature list are being uploaded into the DCS controller. When the transfer of information is complete, you'll see the message "Congratulations, you've added a new engine!" on the screen.

Assigned automatically, your locomotive's name and ID number are now in the ENG menu. Names are abbreviations of the locomotive. For instance, RK M10000 Eng is a Rail-King Union Pacific M-10000 streamliner, and RK RS 27 is a RailKing Soo Line Alco RS-27 diesel.

Click on your locomotive's name with the thumbwheel, and the LCD screen will change to show you an automotive-like digital speedometer, except that the speed is given in O scale miles per hour (shown as SMPH on the screen).

Press the Start Up button on the DCS controller, and your locomotive's steam or diesel sounds roar to life.

With cruise control, if you set train speed at 35 scale mph, your train will maintain that pace.

The controller's thumbwheel has no starting or stopping point.

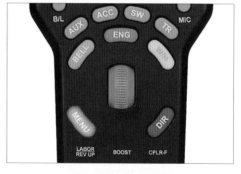

The E-Stop button is an emergency panic button.

Moving out

TMCC has its red dial, and DCS has its thumbwheel. The DCS thumbwheel has no starting or stopping point. If it did, you wouldn't be able to jump from one locomotive to another moving at a different speed in command-control mode.

Each click of the thumbwheel is one scale mph, and the DCS controller's screen shows your progression. There's no blind speed selection as there is with TMCC.

All ProtoSound 2.0 locomotives have cruise control. Set your train speed to 35 scale mph, and the locomotive will stay at a scale 35 mph pace, regardless of the load it is pulling or whether it is going up or down a hill or around a curve.

Direction control and basic sounds

DCS has no neutral. When a locomotive is slowed to zero scale mph, the ProtoSound 2.0 circuitry turns off the power to the locomotive's motor or motors, but the sound system remains on, and all of its features can be operated.

Direction is changed using the DIR button. You can use the DIR button while under way, and your locomotive will slow to a stop, ready to move out in the opposite direction. You can also slow down to zero scale mph and then reverse direction.

The DCS controller has a whistle/horn button, a bell button, and buttons for start-up and shut-down sounds. Additional buttons activate front and rear couplers, boost speed, and apply the brake. Others rev up and rev down diesel motor sounds and turn the smoke generator and headlight on and off.

The controller also has an emergency panic button called E-Stop that halts all of the action.

Jumping between locomotives is menu assisted. Press ENG to display the menu of your locomotives, select the second locomotive you want to operate, and the screen will display that locomotive's name and scale mph indicator. Press ENG again and you can toggle between the two locomotives, or you can return to the main engine menu to select a third locomotive.

The locomotives are listed in the ENG menu by name and an assigned number. You don't have to remember the number, simply select your engine by name.

The ENG menu can be broken into two parts: a list of active locomotives and a list of inactive locomotives. You can freely move locomotives back and forth between the two parts of the list. Keeping only locomotives you are currently using on the active list cuts down on menu clutter. If you have a large roster of ProtoSound 2.0 locomotives, the inactive list is a blessing.

Beyond basic control

While the buttons on the DCS controller give you direct access to the most-used functions (MTH calls this one-touch operation), you can control dozens of other features using menus and the row of soft keys at the top of the controller.

What's on the menu?

DCS uses four primary menus: sound, control, system, and advanced. We cannot cover every feature on every menu, as does the DCS User's Manual, so we'll highlight some of each menu's main features.

The sound menu allows you to control these features:
• Overall volume
• Cab chatter
• Squeaking brakes
• Volume of horn, bell, and other sounds
• Clickety-clack of wheels on rail joints
• Rate of a steam locomotive's chuff sound
• Locomotive volume and pitch as train rounds a layout

The control menu allows you to change smoke volume, activate labored smoke, operate ditch lights, set maximum speed, set acceleration and deceleration rates, and control direction.

By using the advanced menu, you can form lash-ups, create routes, record and play back an operating session, change locomotive sound sets, and reset locomotives.

The system menu focuses on your layout rather than individual locomotive features. You can navigate submenus to add or delete engines, tracks, switches, and accessories. There are also menus that deal with TIU and DCS controller setup and the important track-signal feature (more about that on page 85).

Navigating menus

To remember all of the layers of menus, keep the owner's manual handy. Read it once completely when you first set up DCS and then a second time a few weeks later, when you'll be better able to absorb all of its information. You may even want to index your manual with color-coded file tabs. But don't be intimidated. After a few operating sessions, you'll quickly figure out where the features are that you use most often. And if you become lost, it's easy enough to back out of a menu and move to the correct menu. All of the selections on the menus are described in clear English.

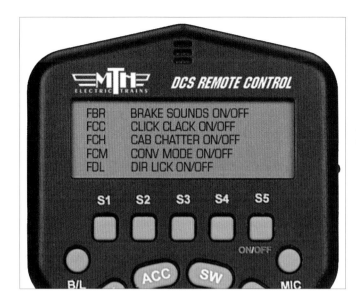

FBR	BRAKE SOUNDS ON/OFF
FCC	CLICK CLACK ON/OFF
FCH	CAB CHATTER ON/OFF
FCM	CONV MODE ON/OFF
FDL	DIR LICK ON/OFF

Function abbreviations can be accessed in a scroll-down menu.

Using soft keys

The soft keys under the controller's screen have different functions depending on which locomotive you are operating.

To guide you, directly above each key, there is a label on the bottom edge of the screen that contains a three-letter abbreviation. By pressing a soft key labeled More, all of the abbreviations will be spelled out on a scroll-down menu.

There is a rhyme and reason to the codes. Sound features start with an S and lighting ones with an L. Menu features that must be set up before activating start with an M, and function features that can be toggled on and off start with an F. For example, LHD turns the headlight on or off, FBR operates the brake, MLU calls up the lash-up menu, and SCS loads the coupler-slack sound.

There is a list of more than 70 of these codes in the back of the DCS manual, but no one locomotive would have all 70 features. Remember, each locomotive has its own unique set of features, depending on whether it is a steam, diesel, or electric locomotive and if it is in the Premier line or the RailKing line.

With only five buttons, you can control dozens of features. As you move through the features, the fifth button is an arrow that point to the right. Press it and the screen shows the next five soft-key features, press the S5 key again and another set is shown, and so on.

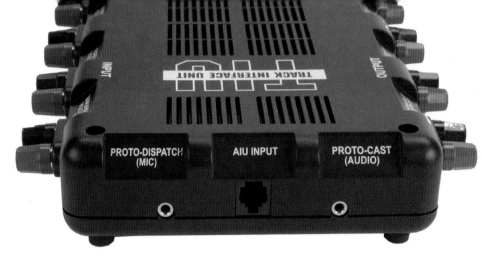

Fun ProtoCast audio features can be operated with a simple connection to the TIU.

Other fun features

There are two DCS sound features that have little to do with railroading but have a lot to do with enjoying your layout.

The first is a microphone. Remember the '70s toy called Mr. Microphone? The DCS controller is a distant relative. Hold down the MIC button on the upper right part of the DCS controller, and speak into the hidden microphone at the very top of the controller. Your voice will be broadcast to the TIU, through the track, into the locomotive, and out its speaker.

The second fun feature also involves broadcasting. The ProtoCast feature allows you to plug a portable cassette or CD player into the TIU and broadcast music instead of engine sounds through the locomotive's speaker.

All for one

Another notable feature is the All function. When operating more than one ProtoSound 2.0 locomotive, selecting the All soft key when the engine menu is displayed sends your DCS controller inputs to all of the locomotives. Press Bell and the bell will ring on all the locomotives. Turn the thumbwheel to 38 scale mph and all of the locomotives will accelerate to 38 scale mph.

Checking signal strength

The DCS signal-strength feature may be the least exciting feature, but it may also be the most important. In the previous chapter, we discussed layout wiring and signal strength. By using the signal-strength feature of a ProtoSound 2.0 locomotive, the locomotive itself can tell you if the signal is adequate or not.

To do so, go to the system menu and select Track Signal. The diesel, steam, or electric sounds coming from your locomotive stop during the signal test.

As your locomotive travels around the layout, the screen on your DCS controller shows a number between 1 and 10. That is the signal strength at that spot of your layout. Ideally, you'll have all 10s, but as long as the signal strength is between 7 and 9, the signal is adequate.

ProtoSound 2.0 locomotives will respond to throttle changes with signal strengths as low as 3 or 2. But signal communication is impaired enough that many other commands will never get through.

Turning off locomotives and your layout

At the end of an operating session, you need to shut down your layout in proper sequence. It's like turning off your home computer – you just can't pull the plug out of the wall.

DCS remembers its settings, so you don't want to shut off the DCS controller without first bringing each and every locomotive down to zero scale mph and then turning off your tracks.

16 Conventional control

The TIU handles all conventional control operation.

MTH's DCS is an all-in-one system. The Track Interface Unit (TIU) contains all the necessary electronics for operating your conventional-controlled prewar, postwar, and modern locomotives while using the DCS handheld controller. There is nothing extra to buy, and there is no extra wiring.

DCS operates conventional-controlled locomotives by raising and lowering track voltage, just like a regular transformer but with the added enjoyment of cordless, walk-around control with a range of about 50 feet.

Another modified wave pattern

DCS uses a modified but filtered electrical wave pattern, so it can operate any conventional-controlled locomotive from any manufacturer – except some of MTH's earliest original ProtoSound-equipped locomotives (built in 1995 and '96) that balk at anything but a pure wave pattern.

To alleviate those problems, MTH has posted step-by-step instructions for operating early ProtoSound locomotives on its Web site. (See "PS1 Engine Transformer Issues" under DCS News.)

Keep in mind that the number of troublesome locomotives is minuscule compared to the number that operate trouble-free in conventional-control mode using the DCS controller. All ProtoSound-equipped locomotives manufactured after 1998 operate just fine using DCS.

Conventional control

When operating DCS in conventional-control mode, you need to use one of the variable-voltage ports.

Using the variable ports

You'll need to use one of the two variable-voltage ports on the TIU to operate locomotives in conventional-control mode. (You use the variable-voltage ports in command-control mode as well, but you first must turn up the track voltage with the DCS controller.)

Remember that the TIU itself needs power, which comes from a transformer plugged into fixed-voltage port number 1 or from a separate, outside source. Depending on your power source, you may need to run jumper wires from fixed-voltage port number 1 to your variable-voltage port on the input side of the TIU.

In conventional-control mode, use the TR menu to select the appropriate track and then use the thumbwheel to raise and lower voltage to the track.

In conventional-control mode, the DCS controller's screen shows a voltage reading instead of a scale mph indicator. Each click of the thumbwheel increases the reading a half-volt. DCS is linear – each click advances voltage the same increment.

A volt isn't a volt

Each click of the thumbwheel moves the voltage indicator on the DCS controller's screen a half-volt. On the track, however, each click is slightly less than a half-volt. The controller is an indicator of track power, but it's not a voltmeter.

Not knowing what power source an operator would use or what voltage it would be set at since some transformers have a slightly higher maximum voltage than others, DCS designers decided it was best to divide the voltage range into 22 parts. So a DCS controller indicating 18 volts is actually allowing $\frac{18}{22}$ of the maximum output of a transformer into the track.

If you have a voltmeter wired into your layout, you'll see

that the DCS controller always indicates a bit more voltage than is really on the track.

The fractional difference really doesn't matter during operation, and the DCS indicator is a useful guide to how much power is on your rails.

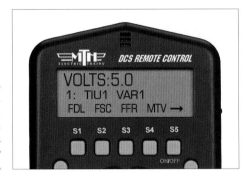

In conventional-control mode, the thumbwheel takes you from 0 volts immediately to 5 volts.

Starting at 5 volts

Conventional-control operation at slow speeds is not DCS's strength. Your first click of the thumbwheel brings the indicator from 0 volts to 5 volts. There are no 1, 2, 3, or 4 volt readings.

That's fine for prewar and postwar locomotives, which usually don't begin to move until track power reaches 7 or more volts.

But modern-era locomotives, with their energy-efficient can-style motors, start moving down the track with only 3 or 4 volts on the rails. Jumping from zero to the DCS-indicated 5 volts makes for an abrupt start, especially if a locomotive is not pulling a load, such as a switcher maneuvering in a yard.

Programming ProtoSound engines

Sound and other conventional-control effects featured in original ProtoSound locomotives can be programmed using DCS. The programming levels, indicated by a series of audio clinks and clanks, are reached by toggling the voltage up or down a specific number of times to reach the appropriate programming level. Just like an MTH Z-4000 transformer, DCS can reach various programming levels without the need to count how many times you have manually toggled the voltage back and forth.

Using the soft keys on the DCS controller, press the MPG key, and scroll through a menu listing of 10 programming options with the thumbwheel. Select an option and DCS will make the appropriate number of voltage toggles for you.

Advanced operation **17**

On a sophisticated layout, such as this one, star wiring works best for DCS.

A large, sophisticated DCS layout needs to be divided into electrical power blocks. But because the DCS signal rides along with the power to the track, each block needs to be backed up by a voltage port of a Track Interface Unit (TIU).

Each TIU has four ports: two fixed-voltage and two variable-voltage. One TIU can handle up to four electrical power blocks, but two of those ports are fixed-voltage only. Should you wish to regulate track voltage in those blocks for conventional-control mode operation, you can't do it with just your DCS controller.

You can control up to five TIUs with a single DCS controller, which equals 20 power blocks. You can go larger, but that requires a second DCS controller.

Since DCS controllers and TIUs continually communicate back and forth with one another, you also are limited by the memory space in the units.

On a sophisticated layout, it is almost essential to follow MTH's suggestion to use star wiring to keep the hot and common wires from the TIU to the track all the same relative length.

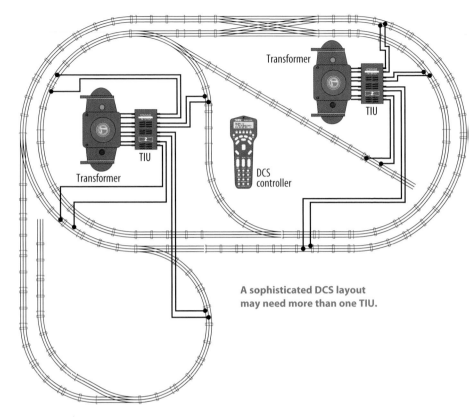

Transformer

TIU

DCS controller

Transformer

TIU

A sophisticated DCS layout may need more than one TIU.

Track switch and accessory control

Small or large, any DCS layout benefits from the addition of an Accessory Interface Unit (AIU).

Each AIU can control up to 10 track switches and up to 10 accessories. You can use up to five AIUs for each TIU. The AIUs connect to a TIU and to each other with a single telephone-style, snap-in cable.

An AIU contains 20 relays all operated by the DCS controller. It is designed to operate all O gauge switches that use three wires (a common wire and wires that activate straight and diverging routes).

On the accessory side, the AIU can activate accessories that turn on through momentary contact, such as MTH's operating gasoline stations, or those that turn on and off like a bedroom light, such as an MTH rotary beacon. The AIU can also activate track uncoupler and activation sections.

MTH has yet to offer a DCS component that controls the speed of motor-driven accessories such as a gantry crane or a log loader.

The AIU is used to activate track switches and accessories.

Names, not numbers

Similar to listing locomotives in the DCS controller's engine roster, you can name your track switches and accessories using an alphanumeric character set. Instead of switch no. 5, the DCS controller's track switch menu can read Hill Branch or Main Yard.

Once you have programmed track switches into your DCS controller, throwing a switch involves only pressing the SW button, scrolling down the menu for the proper switch, and pressing the appropriate soft key for a through route or a diverging route. Straight and curved arrows on the DCS controller's screen tell you which soft key to press for each route.

Selecting names

You can always go back and change the name of a track switch or accessory, but since you need to scroll through the alphanumeric set of characters to select each and every letter of the name, it's best to pick a lasting name on the first try.

You can only use 16 characters per name, so be concise and descriptive. For instance, you don't have to use the word *switch* in the names of your track switches since you need to use the SW menu to get to the names. Use names that can be understood without any explanation.

The same naming suggestion applies for accessories or routes since they also have their own special menus.

Routes and scenes

On sophisticated DCS layouts, it may take five switch throws to direct a locomotive from a roundhouse to a freight yard to pick up a train. You can record those five switch throws and give them a route name using the DCS controller. The next time you wish to move a locomotive from a roundhouse to the freight yard, you can activate the route, and all five switches will throw in appropriate directions.

Recording and activating a route is easy, since the DCS controller's screen prompts you on every move. There's nothing to remember, you just follow the instructions on the screen.

Each DCS controller can remember 15 routes, and each route can control a whopping 250 track switches. DCS also gives you the ability to add or delete a switch to your route without reprogramming the whole route.

You can also program acessory sequences through a scene, which is simply a route for accessories. Each DCS controller can record 15 scenes with 250 movements per scene.

Record and playback

The record and playback feature allows you to record up to 90 minutes, or 500 button pushes of operation, and play it all back.

The possibilities are limited only by your imagination. You can record and play back the simple interaction between a train and accessory – a diesel stops at an animated fueling station, activates its refueling sound effect, and toots its horn twice as it pulls out. Or you can impress visitors with the completely hands-free operation of your layout's trains, track switches, and accessories.

Updating DCS software

DCS is the only O gauge command-control system having software that you can upgrade from your home. It's like upgrading the Internet browser or other software on your home computer. Download an upgrade and replace your old software with a newer version.

Software upgrades and an installer program can be downloaded from MTH's Web site for free. You'll need to connect your TIU to a PC that uses a Windows operating system. Bring along the TIU's transformer and your DCS controller as well. Make the connection using a telephone handset cord, a standard male-to-female serial PC cable, and a ⅛" stereo mini-to-mini cable.

Running TMCC locomotives 18

MTH's DCS can operate its own ProtoSound 2.0 locomotives in command-control mode, and it can operate TMCC-
equipped locomotives in command-control mode. Newer
Lionel Legacy-equipped locomotives can only operate in basic
TMCC mode on a DCS-controlled layout.

Translating languages

The DCS Track Interface Unit (TIU) passes along commands
received from the DCS controller to your layout and to the
ProtoSound 2.0 locomotives on the track. The TIU also trans-
late DCS commands into a language that Lionel's TMCC
system can understand.

If you connect the TIU to a Lionel command base using a
modified DB-9 type computer cable, those translated commands are sent to the command base and then broadcast to
the track. TMCC-equipped locomotives, hearing Lionel's
language, respond in command-control mode. They don't care
that their commands originate from the buttons on a DCS
controller.

How it works

When you operate TMCC-equipped locomotives with a
DCS controller, signals go from the controller to the TIU, just
as if you were controlling a ProtoSound 2.0 locomotive.

But TIU diverts the signal to its TMCC translator,
which sends the signal out its serial port, through the cable,
and into the command base. The command base then
broadcasts the signal through the outside rails of the track –
just as it does in regular TMCC operation. Antennas in
TMCC-equipped locomotives receive the signals, and the
locomotives respond accordingly to the 18 volts of power on
the track.

Running TMCC locomotives

Both at the same time

There is nothing to prevent you from operating a ProtoSound 2.0 locomotive and a TMCC-equipped locomotive each in command-control mode on the same layout at the same time. TMCC signals are broadcast through the outside rail and received by a locomotive's antenna; DCS signals are piggy-backed onto the electrical power flowing through a locomotive. Since each receives a different signal in a different method, there is no conflict. ProtoSound 2.0 locomotives never hear the TMCC signal, and TMCC-equipped locomotives ignore the DCS signal.

A special cable connects the TIU with the TMCC command base.

Necessary equipment

To operate TMCC-equipped locomotives with DCS, in addition to DCS, you will need a Lionel TMCC command base and a special connection cable (MTH part no. 50-1007). While the cable looks like an ordinary DB-9 computer cable, a wire inside is swapped around so that it does not match up with the same connector pins on each end of the cable. The wire connects pin 9 on the TIU side to pin 3 on the command base side, so make sure you install the cable correctly, or it won't work properly.

Adding a TMCC locomotive to your DCS roster

TMCC-equipped locomotives don't transform into Proto-Sound 2.0 locomotives when you put them onto the track of your DCS layout. The TMCC-equipped locomotives retain all of their command-control features.

TMCC-equipped locomotives don't know their names like ProtoSound 2.0 locomotives do. DCS assigns TMCC-equipped locomotives a numeric spot on your roster, and you use an alphanumeric character set to name the locomotive.

TMCC locomotives operate in numbered speed increments, not scale miles per hour.

Using the DCS controller

Operating a TMCC-equipped locomotive with a DCS controller is the same as operating a TMCC-equipped locomotive with a Lionel handheld controller. But instead of turning a red dial, you move the thumbwheel to increase or decrease speed.

The DCS controller does not give a scale mph readout for TMCC-equipped locomotives. Instead, as you move the thumbwheel, it gives you a numeric readout of TMCC speed steps.

The DCS controller features one-touch buttons for whistle/horn, bell, couplers, start-up and shut-down, smoke, boost, brake, and rpm sounds. Other TMCC functions, such as those using the CAB-1 keys Aux-1 and Aux-2, show up on the soft keys at the bottom of the LCD screen.

Operating characteristics

TMCC-equipped locomotives, whether they're made by Lionel, Atlas O, K-Line, 3rd Rail, or Weaver, will operate just fine using the DCS controller. The same goes for postwar Lionel and original MTH ProtoSound-equipped locomotives converted to TMCC control using aftermarket components. The new-generation Lionel Legacy engines will run in basic TMCC mode, but DCS cannot unlock all the features of these locomotives.

Using two controllers

You can use a Lionel TMCC handheld controller and a DCS controller simultaneously. Both send signals to their base units over different frequencies, so there is no chance of interference. In many ways – except for doubling the number of remote controllers to keep track of – you have the best of both worlds. If your layout already uses TMCC and you are adding DCS, you can still operate all of your TMCC-controlled accessories or track switches without rewiring them for DCS.

You can use DCS and TMCC controllers at the same time.

95

19 Additional answers

Because of the sophistication of the DCS system, there is much to discover. The comprehensive, 120-page DCS user's manual does an admirable job of explaining how to operate the DCS controller, the Track Interface Unit (TIU), and ProtoSound 2.0 locomotives in command-control mode. But it's a little skimpy on instructions for non-ProtoSound 2.0 locomotives and set-ups required for large layouts that must have multiple TIUs. Here are some answers to questions you may have on operating DCS.

Must I use star wiring?

Not necessarily. Set up your DCS system and try it first. If you encounter signal problems, it may be best to use star wiring.

Must my track signal strength be 9 or 10?

Ideally, you should at least have a 7, but you can control a moving locomotive on a section of track with a signal strength of 3 or 4. Don't try a communication-heavy function, such as adding a new locomotive, on a section of track with a signal strength of 3 or 4. It almost assuredly won't work.

What does the soft-key abbreviation TVZ mean?

Not all soft-key codes are listed in the back of the user's manual. TVZ is one. If you press the TVZ soft key, the track voltage goes to zero.

How do I reset the TIU circuit breaker?

You must turn off the power and then turn it back on.

Why does my locomotive just sit there when I turn on signal-strength mode?

You must have your locomotive running before entering signal-strength mode.

Can I operate my MTH LocoSound-equipped locomotive in DCS?

Yes, you can operate a RailKing locomotive with LocoSound in DCS but only in conventional-control mode.

I added a ProtoSound 2.0 locomotive to my roster, but something went wrong and not all of the correct information is on the DCS screen. What happened?

If there was a signal problem in the midst of adding a new ProtoSound 2.0 locomotive to your roster, some of the information may have been lost. Delete the "bad" engine from the roster and re-add it to the roster following the steps outlined in the instruction manual.

Can a ProtoSound 2.0 locomotive and a TMCC locomotive be lashed up?

No, you cannot lash up a ProtoSound 2.0 locomotive with a TMCC locomotive, but you can you lash up TMCC locomotives to each other.

Why is there a gap in the numbering of my locomotive roster in the DCS controller?

Early DCS software versions didn't always fully erase deleted locomotives, and some locomotives that were incompletely added to the DCS controller list because of poor signal strength left phantom ID address imprints.

Why do I get an RF Range error (radio frequency) when I'm standing with my DCS controller inches away from the TIU?

The word *range* can sometimes be a misnomer. This error indicates that, regardless of distance, the DCS signal is not coming through clearly.

How can I make sure my DCS controller's signal is getting to the TIU?

Test the DCS controller by connecting it to the TIU with a telephone handset cord.

Why does the red LED on my TIU blink once when I power it up?

It is going through a self-check process.

What is super TIU mode in the system menu?

On a sophisticated DCS layout using more than one TIU, the super mode allows locomotives to move from tracks controlled by one TIU to tracks controlled by a second or third TIU without having to add the locomotive into the software of the additional TIUs.

Where to get more information

In addition to hands-on information from hobby shops and fellow operators, you can find information on DCS in MTH catalogs and in the pages of *Classic Toy Trains* magazine or online at classictoytrains.com. Here are other Web sites that offer DCS information:

- **Mth-railking.com** – MTH's home page contains news items, including DCS news.

- **Protosound2.com** – This offshoot of the main MTH Web site is devoted specifically to Proto-Sound 2.0-equipped locomotives and DCS. MTH offers updated DCS software (and an installer with instructions) that you can download.

- **Ogaugerr.com** – Click on Forum and navigate to the discussion area specifically devoted to DCS.

Glossary

Accessory Interface Unit (AIU): DCS component that throws track switches and activates accessories with a DCS controller.

Accessory Motor Controller (AMC): TMCC component that controls the speed of motor-driven accessories.

Accessory Switch Controller (ASC): TMCC component that throws track switches and activates accessories.

Accessory Voltage Controller (AVC): TMCC component that varies the voltage sent to accessories.

Action Recorder Controller (ARC): TMCC component that records CAB-1 inputs for later playback.

Address: The number assigned to a locomotive, track switch, or accessory that is operated by command control.

Block Power Controller (BPC): TMCC component used to distribute power to track sections.

Bus wiring: Traditional wiring method in which a bus wire runs along the spine of a layout with branches to the track.

CAB-1: First-generation TMCC hand-held controller.

CAB-2: Second-generation TMCC Legacy controller.

Command base: TMCC component that receives a signal from a CAB-1 or CAB-2 and sends it to the track.

Command-control mode: Method of operation in which receiver-equipped locomotives respond to digital signals from a command base instead of moving in response to changes made to track voltage.

Conventional-control mode: Method of operation in which trains respond directly to changes made to track voltage.

Digital Command System (DCS): MTH's command control system.

Electrical power blocks: Dividing a larger layout into separate electrical power sections, each with its own transformer.

ID number: The number assigned to a locomotive, track switch, or accessory that is operated by command control. Same as an address.

Glossary

Legacy: Lionel's second-generation TMCC system, introduced in 2008.

LocoSound: An MTH sound system found in locomotives without DCS receivers.

Operating Track Controller (OTC): TMCC component used to activate operating and uncoupler track sections.

PowerHouse: 135-watt or 180-watt transformer designed for use with TMCC and has no external voltage controllers. Sometimes called bricks because of their shape.

PowerMaster: TMCC component that raises and lowers track voltage when operating conventional-controlled trains with a remote controller. Performs the same basic functions as a TPC.

ProtoSound: MTH's original sound system that was integrated with the control of a locomotive but did not have a command-control receiver.

ProtoSound 2.0: MTH's locomotives equipped with DCS receivers and an integrated speed-control and sound system.

RailSounds: Lionel's sound system that is often integrated with TMCC.

Route: The movement of several track switches recorded and played back with a single keystroke.

SC-2 Switch Controller: TMCC component used to throw track switches and activate accessories with a CAB-1 or CAB-2. Performs the same basic functions as an ASC.

Scene: In DCS, a scene is similar to a route but it involves accessories instead of track switches.

Signal Sounds: Lionel's basic sound system that uses only horn/whistle and bell sounds.

Star wiring: Preferred method for wiring a DCS layout in which the power and return wires radiate from a central point.

Track Interface Unit (TIU): Base unit of DCS system that receives and processes two-way communication between the DCS controller and a ProtoSound 2.0-equipped locomotive.

Track Power Controller (TPC): TMCC component that raises and lowers track voltage when operating conventional-controlled trains.

TrainMaster Command Control (TMCC): Lionel's command control system.

Index

Index

About the author

Neil Besougloff is editor of *Model Railroader* magazine. Previously, he was editor of *Classic Toy Trains* for 10 years. Before that, he was a newspaper journalist for 15 years in Florida and in his native New Jersey. He is slowly but surely building a prewar-style O gauge layout after moving to a new home in Oconomowoc, Wisc. Neil and his wife Susy are the parents of five boys. In addition to toy trains, Neil spends his free time reading history books and tinkering with his 1931 Ford Model A.

Carl Swanson succeeded Neil Besougloff as editor of *Classic Toy Trains*. At Kalmbach Publishing Co. for 12 years, Carl also worked for *Model Railroader* and *Trains* as well as an earlier stint on CTT. Carl was also the founding editor of *RailNews* magazine and served as editor of *Passenger Train Journal* prior to joining Kalmbach. An avid model railroader, Carl has an 8 x 12-foot O gauge layout in his Milwaukee home, where he lives with his wife Judy, sons John and Daniel, and daughter Rachel.

Acknowledgments
Thanks to Andy Edleman and Melissa Shipley of MTH for providing photos.

Expert Tips ...

to get your model railroads up and running!

You'll find 16 realistic, themed layout plans, each including track diagrams, wiring schemes, and a list of suggested equipment in this book.
10-8350 • $18.95

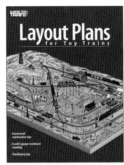

Features layout descriptions, track requirements, operating suggestions, and track plans for layouts that will fit bedroom to basement-sized space.
10-8275 • $15.95

Includes techniques and steps for lubrication, troubleshooting, and the right way to replace tires, batteries, and light bulbs.
10-8327 • $17.95

Provides an overview of the various lines of sectional and flexible track, and demonstrates how to cut, bend, wire, and install track into your layouts.
10-8365 • $19.95